GOOD
MORNINGS

GREAT BREAKFASTS AND BRUNCHES

FOR STARTING THE DAY RIGHT

GOOD
MORNINGS

BY MICHAEL MC LAUGHLIN

PHOTOGRAPHY BY DAN CLARK

CHRONICLE BOOKS

SAN FRANCISCO

Library of Congress Cataloging-in-Publication Data:
McLaughlin, Michael.
      Good mornings: great breakfasts and brunches for starting the day right/
  by Michael McLaughlin.
          p.   cm.
     Includes index.
     ISBN 0-8118-1181-6
     1. Breakfasts. 2. Brunches. I. Title.
TX733.M477 1996
641.5'2—dc20   95-42368
                                         CIP

Printed in Hong Kong.

Book design by Gerald Reis & Company Design; food styling by Kathleen Fazio.

Marie Simmons's Dark Ginger Bread, Lemon Slice Sauce, and Blueberry Crumb Buns are from *Classic Home Desserts,* by Richard Sax. Copyright © 1994 by Richard Sax. Reprinted by permission of Chapters Publishing Ltd. All rights reserved.

Selma Brown Morrow's Cheese Blintzes with Fruit Sauce from *Bon Appétit* magazine. *Bon Appétit* is a registered trademark of Advance Magazine Publishers, Inc., published through its division The Condé Nast Publications Inc. Copyright © 1995 by The Condé Nast Publications Inc. Reprinted with permission.

Cafe Pasqual's Red Chile Sauce and Pasqual's Pan-Fried Polenta with Chorizo and Corn are from *Cafe Pasqual's Cookbook,* by Katharine Kagel. Copyright © 1993 by Katharine Kagel. Reprinted by permission of Chronicle Books.

The photographer wishes to thank the following in San Francisco for the use of their beautiful wares: Fred and Patty at Maison d'etre for use of their personal collection, my friends Jane and Robert at Summer House Gallery, and Fillamento. Thanks also to Tony at Gerald Reis Design for his help and quiet humor. And finally, thanks to my loving and supportive wife, Laura, and our two kids, Ellis and Paris.

Distributed in Canada by Raincoast Books
8680 Cambie Street
Vancouver, B.C. V6P 6M9

10 9 8 7 6 5 4 3 2

Chronicle Books
85 Second Street
San Francisco, CA 94105

INTRODUCTION—GOOD MORNING! OUR TWIN SUBJECTS ARE BREAKFAST AND BRUNCH, SEPARATE BUT EQUAL SIDES OF THE CULINARY COIN THAT ARE A.M. FOOD. I WILL NOT BEGIN BY DECLARING THESE MEALS THE MOST IMPORTANT OF THE DAY, SINCE I DO NOT BELIEVE THERE ARE ANY *UNIMPORTANT* MEALS. RATHER I ASSERT THAT OF THE THREE (OR MORE) IMPORTANT MEALS ONE CAN MANAGE, WITH DEFT SCHEDULING, TO PACK INTO A DAY, BREAKFAST AND BRUNCH ARE NEARLY ALWAYS THE FIRST, AND SO, DUE TO THEIR LEADOFF POSITION, NECESSARILY AND PROPERLY DESERVE THE CONCENTRATED ATTENTION OF ANYONE WHO IS SERIOUS ABOUT EATING. (IF YOU ARE NOT SERIOUS ABOUT EATING, YOU HAVE PURCHASED THIS BOOK BY MISTAKE, AND SHOULD BE ABLE, IF YOU HAVE SAVED THE SALES SLIP, TO RETURN IT AND GET YOUR MONEY BACK. IF YOU ARE SERIOUS ABOUT EATING BUT DO NOT EAT EITHER BREAKFAST OR BRUNCH, YOU HAVE BEEN OVERLOOKING EXTRAORDINARY DAILY OPPORTUNITIES, BUT HAVE FORTUNATELY STUMBLED ACROSS A PASSIONATE GUIDE THAT I BELIEVE WILL CHANGE YOUR LIFE.) THESE ARE BIG, BOLD BREAKFASTS AND BRUNCHES, THE SAME KIND OF TERRIFICALLY INTERESTING, WELL-MADE FOOD THAT I LIKE TO EAT AT ALL THE OTHER MEALS OF MY DAY. ENJOYED SOLO OR DISHED OUT TO A HUNGRY CROWD, THESE DISHES HAVE A FROM-SCRATCH APPEAL MISSING FROM PRE-FAB, FAST-FOOD BREAKFASTS, AND, INDEED, FROM TOO MANY MEALS NOWADAYS, NO MATTER WHAT TIME OF DAY THEY ARE SERVED. THEY ARE NOT (ALL) SPICY, OR RICH, OR OFFBEAT, BUT NEITHER ARE THEY MERE BLAND, NUTRITIONAL FODDER. COOK AND EAT ONE OF THESE HEARTY BREAKFASTS OR BRUNCHES, AND YOU MAY HAVE A HARD TIME CONCENTRATING ON THE FUNNY PAPERS, MIGHT EVEN FIND YOURSELF WHISTLING WHILE YOU WORK, AND YOU WILL CERTAINLY LOOK FORWARD TO WAKING UP TOMORROW WITH A LOT MORE ANTICIPATION THAN YOU DID TODAY.

WITHIN A COMFORTABLY RITUALIZED FRAMEWORK—CEREAL, EGGS, POTATOES, PANCAKES, SMOKY MEATS AND FISH, TOAST MAYBE, A LITTLE FRUIT, A CUP OF COFFEE—BREAKFAST STILL MANAGES TO BE A MEAL THAT VARIES WIDELY FROM COAST TO COAST, FROM PERSON TO PERSON. FOR EACH STACK OF BLUE-BERRY PANÇAKES SERVED THERE'S A PLATE OF GARLICKY LINGUINE SCRAMBLED WITH EGGS; FOR EVERY HAM AND CHEDDAR OMELET THERE'S ONE WITH HAM, BRIE, AND WILD MUSHROOMS. CRISP HOME FRIES MAY BE THE TRADITIONAL STARCH-ON-THE-SIDE, OR FIERY GIZZARD-SPANGLED DIRTY RICE MAY DO THE TRICK. FOR EVERYONE LIFTING A BRAN MUFFIN THERE'S SOMEONE ELSE LIFTING A SPICY BREAKFAST TACO. GET TO THE POINT, YOU SAY, YOU'RE HUNGRY? THE IMPORTANT THING IS NOT WHAT YOUR BREAKFAST CONSISTS OF (JAMES BEARD ONCE RECOMMENDED FETTUCCINE ALFREDO, NOT A BAD IDEA), BUT THAT IT NOT BE A BORE AND THAT YOU ENJOY WHATEVER IT IS WITH GUSTO. IF YOU'VE LATELY FOUND YOUR BREAKFAST FRAMEWORK A LITTLE <u>TOO</u> RITUALIZED, THE FOLLOWING EIGHT CHAPTERS WILL PROVIDE YOU WITH PLENTY OF MORNING FOOD FOR THOUGHT, A NEW RITUAL IN THE MAKING. FINALLY, IF YOU'RE NO SHORT ORDER COOK AND FINDING TIME FOR MAKING BREAKFAST IS AN ISSUE (PRESUMABLY WHY THE EGG MCMUFFIN EXISTS), THE RECIPES CONTAIN, WHEREVER POSSIBLE, DO-AHEAD STEPS THAT WILL LET YOU GET MUCH OF THE WORK OUT OF THE WAY THE NIGHT BEFORE. NOW LET'S GET CRACKING!

BREAKFAST

CEREAL, GRANOLA, AND PORRIDGE

1

Granola-Berry Parfait—page 13

Cherry-Almond Granola

Makes about 8 cups

Homemade granola is nearly always fresher than what you can buy, and since it's a casual and forgiving thing to stir together, the cook's whim is the rule of the day. Stick to the basic proportions, but feel free to add (or delete) various nuts, dried fruits, and flavoring elements as desired. The sweet, crunchy results can be enjoyed in a bowl at breakfast (naturally), but serve equally well as a pancake additive (page 30) or as a snack.

½ **cup packed light brown sugar**
¼ **cup unsulphured molasses**
¼ **cup honey**
¼ **cup water**
3 **tablespoons canola or other flavorless oil**
3 **cups old-fashioned rolled oats**
1 **cup dried pitted tart cherries or dried cranberries**
1 **cup coarsely chopped unblanched almonds**
½ **cup raw pumpkin seeds**
⅓ **cup unsweetened dried flaked coconut**
⅓ **cup raw hulled sunflower seeds**
¼ **cup wheat germ**
2 **tablespoons unhulled sesame seeds**

- Position a rack in the middle of the oven and preheat to 325 degrees F.
- In a small, heavy saucepan over medium heat, stir together the brown sugar, molasses, honey, water, and canola oil and bring just to a boil.
- Meanwhile, in a roasting pan stir together all the remaining ingredients. Gradually pour the hot syrup over the oat mixture, stirring constantly to moisten evenly. Set the roasting pan in the oven and bake the granola, stirring occasionally, until it is lightly but evenly browned and slightly crunchy, about 40 minutes.
- Remove from the oven and let the granola cool in the pan on a rack, stirring once or twice (it will become crunchier as it cools). Store at room temperature in an airtight container.

Cinnamon-Raisin Risotto

Serves 4

The great Italian dish of slowly simmered short grain (Arborio) rice, creamily sauced by the starch-thickened liquid in which it is cooked, nicely adapts for breakfast. Simmered in cinnamon-infused milk and studded with plump raisins, this breakfast risotto resembles a moist, not-too-sweet rice pudding. Serve it with a sprinkle of sugar, plus a pat of butter, if desired. In the best risottos, the grains remain slightly al dente. At this hour of the day I prefer things a little more tender, and so I cook the rice completely.

- In a saucepan over low heat, combine the water, milk, cinnamon stick, and salt. Bring to a simmer and keep at a very low simmer.
- In a heavy saucepan over low heat, melt the butter. Add the rice and stir until well coated with butter, about 1 minute. Stir 1½ cups of the simmering milk mixture and the raisins into the rice. Simmer, stirring occasionally, until almost all the liquid is absorbed, about 7 minutes. Add ½ cup of the simmering milk mixture and continue to simmer, stirring occasionally, until almost all the liquid is absorbed, about 5 minutes. Stir in another ½ cup of the simmering milk mixture and transfer the cinnamon stick from the milk pan to the rice pan. Continue adding the milk mixture, ½ cup at a time, until the rice is just tender and creamily sauced, about 45 minutes' total cooking time (the time varies widely depending upon the age of the rice used and the altitude of your kitchen). Should you use up all of the milk mixture before the rice is tender, continue adding plain simmering water, not more milk.
- Discard the cinnamon stick. Spoon the risotto into warmed bowls and serve immediately, offering sugar and butter at the table.

3 cups water
2 cups milk
1 cinnamon stick, 2½ inches long
3 tablespoons unsalted butter
1 cup Italian Arborio rice (do not rinse)
½ cup dark or golden raisins
Granulated or brown sugar and unsalted butter, for serving
Pinch of salt

Granola-Berry Parfait

Serves 1

Breakfast "parfaits"—layered concoctions of granola, yogurt, and fruit assembled in tall, stemmed glasses—have caught on partly because the dessert-inspired name is so self-indulgent, and partly because of the textural fun to be had by digging down through the various juicy, crunchy, and creamy strata. This version is only a guideline, not a hard-and-fast recipe: Use any type granola you like, substitute flavored yogurt if desired, and choose whatever breakfast-appropriate fruit is in seasonal perfection.

- In a small bowl, whisk together the yogurt, honey, and vanilla. Spoon about one-third of the granola into the bottom of a stemmed 12-ounce glass. Spoon about one-third of the yogurt mixture over the granola. Sprinkle about half the berries over the yogurt. Repeat with the remaining ingredients, ending with a yogurt layer.
- Garnish the parfait with the extra berries, stick a long-handled spoon into the glass, and serve immediately.

¾ cup plain yogurt, regular or nonfat
2 tablespoons honey
¼ teaspoon vanilla extract
½ cup granola
½ cup blueberries, picked over, plus a few extra berries for garnish

Creole Rice Fritters with Blackberry Sauce

Serves 6

New Orleans loves donutlike *calas*, lavishly dusted with confectioners' sugar and enjoyed with a mid-morning cup of strong chicory-laced coffee. Try them that way by all means, or do as I do, and serve them (very hot!) in a pool of blackberry sauce, alone or as an accompaniment to ham and eggs. This recipe is adapted from Alex Patout's *Patout's Cajun Home Cooking*.

1½ **cups water**
⅔ **cup converted rice**
½ **teaspoon salt**
⅔ **cup unbleached all-purpose flour**
¼ **cup granulated sugar**
3 **eggs**
1 **package (2½ teaspoons) active dry yeast**
2 **teaspoons minced orange zest (colored peel)**
¼ **teaspoon freshly grated nutmeg**
Vegetable oil for deep-frying
Fresh Blackberry Sauce (page 70), heated to a simmer
Confectioners' sugar, in a sieve

The Night Before

■ In a small, heavy saucepan over high heat, bring the water to a boil. Stir in the rice and ¼ teaspoon of the salt, lower the heat, cover, and cook until the rice is tender and steam holes have appeared in the surface, about 20 minutes. Transfer the rice to a bowl, fluff it with a fork, and let cool to room temperature. Cover and refrigerate.

In the Morning

■ In a large bowl, toss together the rice, flour, and granulated sugar. In a small bowl, stir together the eggs, yeast, orange zest, nutmeg, and the remaining ¼ teaspoon salt. Stir the egg mixture into the rice mixture. Cover with a clean towel and let the fritter batter stand at room temperature until foamy, about 1 hour.

■ Position a rack in the middle of the oven and preheat to 250 degrees F. Line a jelly roll pan with several thicknesses of paper towels.

■ Pour at least 1 inch of vegetable oil into a large, deep skillet and heat to 375 degrees F. Stir the batter well. Working in batches to avoid lowering the temperature of the oil, drop the rice by 3 tablespoon dollops into the hot oil. Cook until richly browned and crisp, turning the fritters once at the halfway point, about 2 minutes' total cooking time. With a slotted spoon, transfer to the jelly roll pan and keep warm in the oven.

■ When all the fritters are done, spoon about ⅓ cup sauce onto each of 6 plates. Set 3 fritters onto each puddle of sauce. Sprinkle heavily with confectioners' sugar and serve immediately.

Cornmeal Mush with Warm Ginger-Pear Compote

Serves 4

If it helps you decide to make this utterly comforting, stick-to-the-ribs bowl of goodness, think of it as polenta instead of mush, which, I must admit, has a bit of a PR problem. For the best texture use coarsely ground meal, and, for company, consider stirring up to ¼ cup of the rich Italian cream cheese called mascarpone into the mush, in place of the butter.

- In a heavy saucepan over medium heat, whisk the water gradually into the cornmeal. Whisk in the salt. Bring to a simmer, then cover partially and cook, stirring often, until thick, about 40 minutes.
- Remove from the heat and stir the butter into the mush. Divide the mush among 4 bowls. Top the mush with the pear compote (use up to ½ cup per person) and serve immediately.

5 cups cold water
1¼ cups coarse yellow cornmeal, preferably stone-ground
¼ teaspoon salt
2 tablespoons unsalted butter
Ginger-Pear Compote (page 74), heated to a simmer

Many-Grain Porridge with Apple Butter and Yogurt

Serves 6

If the term porridge (not to mention gruel) produces in you a grim, Oliver Twist–inspired shudder, please consider the following. Complex of color, texture, and above all flavor, it is a nutritional powerhouse—just the sort of breakfast that will have everyone asking for "more, please." During summer months, I increase the amount of water by one cup, and enjoy the leftover porridge cold and straight from the refrigerator on succeeding days, topped with buttermilk and a generous sprinkle of brown sugar—a fine hot weather breakfast. Millet, flaxseed, and steel-cut oats are available in health-food stores.

- In a heavy saucepan over high heat, bring the water to a boil. Add the Jubilee, millet, barley, wild rice, flaxseed, and salt. Partially cover the pan, lower the heat, and simmer, stirring once or twice, for 15 minutes. Stir in the raisins and the steel-cut oats and continue to simmer, stirring often, until the porridge is thick and the grains are tender, about 30 minutes.
- Spoon the hot porridge into bowls. Top each serving with a generous dollop each of apple butter and yogurt and serve immediately.

6½ cups water
⅓ cup Lundberg Family Jubilee or other mixed fancy rice blend, rinsed
⅓ cup millet, rinsed
⅓ cup whole-grain (not pearl) barley, rinsed
⅓ cup wild rice, rinsed
2 tablespoons flaxseed
½ teaspoon salt
½ cup dark or golden raisins or pitted tart dried cherries
⅓ cup steel-cut (or Irish) oats
About 1½ cups apple butter, preferably unsweetened
About 1½ cups plain yogurt, regular or nonfat

EGGS

92

Three-Minute Eggs with Tarragon Butter—page 25

Egg Eyes

Serves 1 or 2

Use white sandwich bread and serve this child-pleasing arrangement of egg and toast with bacon or sausage if you like. Or emulate Olympia Dukakis, frying one up for daughter Cher in the film *Moonstruck*: make it with slices of crusty Italian-style bread, and garnish the plate with roasted red peppers (a fine light supper with a glass of red wine).

2 thin slices firm white sandwich bread, each about 4 inches square
4 tablespoons (½ stick) unsalted butter
2 medium eggs, at room temperature
Salt
Freshly ground black pepper

- Using a round cutter 3 inches in diameter, cut out a hole in the center of each slice of bread; reserve the cut-out round.
- In a large, preferably nonstick skillet over medium heat, melt the butter. When it foams, add the bread slices and the cut-out rounds and cook, rearranging them in the skillet to promote even toasting, until golden brown on the bottom, 2 to 3 minutes. Turn the slices and the rounds. Break an egg into the hole in each slice of bread. Cover the skillet and cook, carefully rearranging the bread slices and rounds in the skillet to promote even cooking, until the eggs are done to your liking, about 3 minutes for sunny-side up and rather soft. Or carefully turn the bread slices and cook another minute or two for over easy.
- Transfer to a plate or plates, season to taste with salt and pepper, and serve immediately.

Shirred Eggs with Ham

Serves 4

Shirred eggs are baked uncovered, producing a subtly different result—firmer, with a crisp edge—from eggs enclosed and coddled. Cooked atop a thick slice of ham, these are most of the meal (just add Creamed Hash Browns, page 60, and toast) and, like coddled eggs, a convenient way to feed a crowd. I buy boneless delicatessen ham in round slices that, when slashed around the edge, just fit my round gratin dishes, providing tidy cups in which to bake the eggs. If your dishes differ, rearrange your ham accordingly.

¾ pound baked ham, cut into 4 round slices
8 eggs
4 tablespoons (½ stick) unsalted butter, melted
Freshly ground black pepper

- Position a rack in the middle of the oven and preheat to 350 degrees F.
- Cut six or eight 1-inch slashes around the ham slices. Press each ham slice into a round gratin dish 3½ inches in diameter. Crack 2 eggs into each ham-lined dish. Drizzle the yolks of the eggs with the butter, dividing it evenly and using it all.
- Set the dishes on the oven rack and bake until done to your liking, about 15 minutes for eggs that have just-set whites and liquid yolks.
- Remove from the oven, season with pepper (the ham juices usually provide enough salt), and serve immediately.

Huevos Chimayó

Serves 4

Here is my improvisation upon traditional southwestern *huevos rancheros*—fried eggs set atop corn tortillas and napped with a sauce of green chiles and tomatoes. Celebrating the fine red chiles grown and dried around the small northern New Mexico town of Chimayó, and utilizing the more common flour tortillas of the region, this variation remains a fine and not-too-spicy way to begin the day. Eggs fried sunny-side up are the norm (and as they slide out of the skillet, one perfectly round pair at a time, they neatly fit atop the tortillas), but scramble, poach, or otherwise cook them any way you like.

- Position a rack in the middle of the oven and preheat to 350 degrees F.
- Evenly spread one side of each tortilla with the beans, dividing them evenly and using them all scatter the cheese evenly over the beans, dividing it evenly and using it all. Working in batches timed to the frying of the eggs, lay the tortillas, cheese side up, on a baking sheet. Set the sheet in the oven and bake the tortillas just until the beans are heated through and the cheese is melted, about 5 minutes.
- Meanwhile, in a small saucepan over low heat, warm the red chile sauce, stirring often, until simmering.
- To fry the eggs, in a nonstick 6-inch skillet over medium heat, melt ½ tablespoon of the butter. Crack 2 eggs into the skillet. With a rubber scraper, carefully stir the whites, without breaking the yolks, to promote even cooking. Cover the skillet and cook the eggs until the whites are set but not browned, 2 to 3 minutes for sunny-side up. Or fry for 2 minutes, then flip and fry for another 1 or 2 minutes for over easy. Season lightly with salt and freshly ground pepper.
- Set 1 tortilla on a plate. Slide the eggs out of the skillet onto the tortilla. Spoon about one-fourth of the sauce over the eggs. Sprinkle one-fourth of the onions over the sauce. Serve immediately. Repeat with the remaining ingredients.

4 thick flour tortillas, preferably whole wheat, each 6 inches in diameter

¾ cup canned refried beans, preferably black beans

6 ounces jalapeño jack cheese, shredded

1 cup Cafe Pasqual's Red Chile Sauce (page 70)

2 tablespoons unsalted butter

8 eggs

Salt

Freshly ground black pepper

2 green onions, thinly sliced

Hangtown Fry

Serves 2

This dish is named for a California gold rush town (now called Placerville), and memorializes the expensive meal ordered up there by a legendary miner who had just struck it rich. In my version, the dish is rendered as a bacon omelet, topped with crisp deep-fried oysters. Enliven the rich dish by shaking on plenty of hot sauce.

½ **pound (about 6 strips) thick-sliced bacon**
6 eggs
Salt
Freshly ground black pepper
Vegetable oil for deep-frying
⅓ **cup unbleached all-purpose flour**
⅓ **cup coarse yellow cornmeal, preferably stoneground**
6 large oysters, shucked and drained

- Lay the bacon strips in a large, heavy skillet. Set the skillet over medium heat and cook the bacon, turning the strips once or twice, until brown and crisp, 8 to 10 minutes. Reserve 3 tablespoons of the bacon drippings. Coarsely chop the bacon.
- In each of 2 small bowls, break 3 of the eggs. Add a pinch of salt and a grinding of pepper to each bowl and whisk briefly with a fork.
- Pour vegetable oil into a deep fryer or heavy saucepan to fill no more than halfway full and heat to 375 degrees F. Meanwhile, on a plate, stir together the flour, cornmeal, ½ teaspoon salt, and ½ teaspoon pepper. Dredge the oysters in the seasoned flour. Carefully lower the oysters into the hot oil and cook, stirring once or twice, until crisp and golden, about 1 minute. With a slotted spoon, transfer the oysters to paper towels to drain.
- Meanwhile, in a 6-inch, preferably nonstick omelet pan over medium heat, warm half the reserved bacon drippings. When hot, add one batch of seasoned eggs and cook, stirring them once or twice with a rubber scraper or a wooden spoon, until they just begin to coagulate, about 1 minute. Stir in half the bacon and continue to cook, shaking the pan horizontally over the heat and loosening the eggs around the edge, until the center of the omelet is almost, but not quite, done to your liking, another 1 to 2 minutes. Tilt the skillet over a warmed plate and encourage the omelet to roll out onto it in an oval shape. Arrange 3 fried oysters atop the omelet and serve immediately. Repeat with the remaining ingredients.

Scrambled Eggs with Asparagus

Serves 4

This simple recipe illustrates the basic method for scrambling eggs, whether or not other ingredients find their way into the skillet. I like striations of white and yolk in my scrambled eggs and thus limit my whisking before cooking to four or five light strokes with a fork. Other cooks may wish to whip the eggs vigorously until fully blended—your choice. Doneness, too, is a matter of taste. When scrambling for a crowd I've been known to take orders, spooning out early portions for the soft and runny fans (me foremost), while continuing to cook the remaining eggs until firm for the others.

The Night Before

- Bring a large pot three-fourths full of water to a boil. Add the asparagus and 1 tablespoon salt to the boiling water and cook uncovered, stirring once or twice, until just tender, about 4 minutes. Drain and immediately transfer to a large bowl of ice water. Let stand, stirring once or twice, until cold, then drain well. Wrap and refrigerate.

In the Morning

- Let the asparagus come to room temperature.
- In a large bowl, whisk together the eggs, ¾ teaspoon salt, and the pepper.
- In a large, preferably nonstick skillet over medium heat, melt the butter. When it foams, add the eggs and asparagus and cook, stirring often, until just set while remaining moist, about 4 minutes, or until done to your liking. Serve immediately.

1 bunch (about 1 pound) asparagus, trimmed, peeled, and cut into ½-inch lengths
Salt
Ice water
10 eggs
½ teaspoon freshly ground black pepper
4 tablespoons (½ stick) unsalted butter

Mushroom Forager's Omelets

Serves 2

Morels, the delicious wild mushrooms that are in season for only a short time, are elusive, and a hunter might spend hours to gather only a handful. (Those of us who forage for them in gourmet shops may also come home minimally supplied, since morels routinely retail for as much as forty dollars a pound.) One of the best ways of getting the most mileage out of the fewest morels are these delicious omelets, which can be made, should you come home totally empty-handed, with ordinary cultivated mushrooms.

- In a large, heavy skillet over medium heat, melt 2 tablespoons of the butter. Add the ham and cook, stirring occasionally, until lightly browned, 8 to 10 minutes. Add the morels, season with a pinch of salt, cover, and cook, stirring once or twice, until just tender, 8 to 10 minutes.
- Meanwhile, into each of 2 small bowls, break 3 of the eggs. Add a pinch of salt and a grinding of pepper to each bowl and whisk briefly with a fork for a rougher-textured omelet, or longer for a smoother omelet.
- In a heavy, 6-inch, preferably nonstick omelet pan over medium heat, melt half the remaining butter. When it foams, add 1 batch of whisked eggs. Cook the eggs, stirring often with a rubber scraper, until they begin to set into a solid layer, about 1 minute. Scatter half the Brie over the eggs. Spoon half the ham mixture over the Brie. When the omelet is done to your liking (about 1 minute longer for medium-soft), tilt the skillet over a warmed plate and encourage the omelet to roll out onto it into an oval shape. Serve immediately. Repeat with the remaining ingredients.

4 tablespoons (½ stick) unsalted butter
3 ounces well-trimmed baked smoked ham, diced
6 ounces fresh morels, picked over and sliced crosswise into ¼-inch-thick rounds
Salt
6 eggs
Freshly ground black pepper
2 ounces ripe triple-crème Brie cheese, rind included, cut into small pieces, at room temperature

Within certain sensible parameters of flavor compatibility, texture, and A.M. appropriateness (your breakfast, your call), the list of filling possibilities, alone or in combination, is almost unlimited. Here, to provoke thought and stimulate creativity at a time of day when either can be difficult to summon, are some restaurant combinations that have pleased me, along with some others of my own devising.

- Lox, potatoes, and sautéed onions; toasted bagel on the side, from Barney Greengrass in New York City

- Bacon, sharp English Cheddar, and chopped raw spinach (which wilts under the heat of the eggs), from Elephant and Castle in New York City

- Roast turkey and bacon rolled into the omelet, Swiss cheese melted on top, avocado slices as garnish, from Claire's in Catalina, Arizona

- Strips of cooked chicken, strips of crisp-fried corn tortilla, diced tomatoes, green chiles, and jack cheese (all inside), from The Blue Willow in Tucson

- Peaches sautéed in unsalted butter with fresh lemon juice and brown sugar, inside the omelet along with drained ricotta cheese

- Mixed mushrooms sautéed in unsalted butter with tarragon, then finished with a little cream and Dijon mustard before being rolled into the omelet

- Sautéed diced ham, sautéed diced unpeeled apples, and Gouda cheese, all inside the omelet

- Fresh corn kernels and juices cooked with a little green onion and unsalted butter until thick (inside), sour cream and hot salsa on top

- Blanched broccoli (not too crisp), roasted sweet pepper strips, and shredded smoky provolone, all inside

- Leftover ratatouille and mild fresh goat cheese (both inside)

- Chopped tomatoes sautéed in unsalted butter (garlic optional) until they thicken and lose their watery quality, and lots of chopped fresh basil, all inside the omelet

- Chunked ripe pears sautéed in unsalted butter with a touch of maple syrup plus diced smoked turkey breast (all inside); pumpernickel or rye toast on the side.

- Gruyère cheese and toasted walnuts (both inside)

Poached Eggs and Fried Tomatoes with Creamy Ham Sauce

Serves 4

A twist on eggs Benedict, with touches of the deep South, the creamy, smoky thyme-scented sauce that naps this dish will be at its best made with the finest dry-cured Smithfield-type country ham you can find. Thick-sliced premium English muffins (like those from the Wolferman's Bakery, see Mail-Order Sources) are my first choice for supporting player in this enterprise, but squares of your favorite corn bread, or even the panfried polenta on page 101 all work wonderfully well, too.

½ cup coarse yellow cornmeal

1 teaspoon freshly ground black pepper

1½ cups whipping cream

¼ pound well-trimmed firm, smoky ham, cut into ¼-inch dice

1 tablespoon minced fresh thyme, plus thyme sprigs for garnish (optional)

2 tablespoons fresh lemon juice

4 tablespoons (½ stick) unsalted butter

2 large, firm but ripe tomatoes, cut into 8 thick slices

2 teaspoons salt

8 eggs

4 thick English muffins, split and lightly toasted

■ On a plate, stir together the cornmeal and ½ teaspoon of the pepper. Set aside.

■ In a small, heavy saucepan over medium heat, combine the cream, ham, and minced thyme. Bring to a boil, then lower the heat and simmer uncovered, stirring once or twice, until reduced to 1 cup, about 20 minutes. Remove from the heat and stir in the lemon juice and the remaining ½ teaspoon pepper. Cover and keep warm.

■ In a large skillet over medium heat, melt the butter. Dredge the tomatoes in the prepared cornmeal and fry them in the skillet, turning them once, until lightly browned and crisp, about 4 minutes per side.

■ Meanwhile, to a deep skillet, add water to a depth of 2 inches. Set over medium heat and bring just to a simmer. Stir in the salt. One at a time, break the eggs into a small dish and then slide them into the water. Adjust the heat to keep the water from exceeding a simmer and cook the eggs, gently shaping them into ovals with a spoon, to the desired doneness, about 3 minutes for medium-firm.

■ Arrange 2 muffin halves on each of 4 plates. Top each half with 1 fried tomato slice. With a slotted spoon, remove the eggs from the water, blot briefly on paper towels, and set an egg atop each tomato slice. Spoon the cream sauce over and around the eggs and muffins, garnish each serving with a sprig of thyme if desired, and serve immediately.

Scrambled Eggs with Garlicky Linguine

Serves 4 to 6

Among those dishes for which starchy leftovers are frugally tossed into scrambled eggs, producing a second, unique, and unexpected meal, Jewish eggs and matzo (matzo brei) and Mexican eggs and corn tortilla chips (migas) come immediately to mind. Less expected but no less interesting and far livelier from the morning adventurer's point of view, is this egg-and-pasta combo, inspired by a dish from Hugo's in West Hollywood. Serve it with a grilled sausage link, Italian or otherwise, and a hunk of toasted semolina bread. Or transform it into an informal but satisfying supper by napping it with a big spoonful of excellent tomato sauce.

The Night Before

- Fill a large pot with at least 3 quarts of water and bring to a boil. Add the linguine and 1 tablespoon salt and cook, stirring occasionally, until the pasta is very tender, about 9 minutes. Drain the pasta and rinse it well under cold running water. Toss the pasta with the olive oil, cover, and refrigerate.

In the Morning

- In a large bowl, lightly whisk the eggs with ¾ teaspoon salt and the black pepper.
- In a large skillet over medium heat, melt the butter. Add the garlic and crushed red pepper and cook without allowing the garlic to brown, stirring often, for 4 minutes. Add the linguine and cook, stirring often, until heated through and flavored with garlic, about 4 minutes.
- Add the eggs and cook, stirring often, until they are set to your liking, 4 to 5 minutes for fairly soft eggs. Remove skillet from heat, stir in Parmigiano, and serve immediately.

6 **ounces dried semolina linguine, preferably imported**
Salt
1 **tablespoon olive oil**
10 **eggs**
½ **teaspoon freshly ground black pepper**
6 **tablespoons (¾ stick) unsalted butter**
2 **garlic cloves, minced**
¼ **teaspoon crushed red pepper**
⅓ **cup grated Parmigiano Reggiano cheese**

Three-Minute Eggs with Tarragon Butter
Serves 1

This is a lovely, simple thing: soft, custardy eggs topped with a melting puddle of green-flecked, anise-scented butter. It's a light, elegant breakfast, needing only crisp, dry toast for dunking into the eggs. Three things to know about three-minute eggs: pricking the shell prevents breakage, cold eggs take longer to cook than room-temperature eggs, and at an altitude of seven thousand feet, a three-minute egg can easily take more like six.

The Night Before

- In a small bowl, combine the tarragon and salt. With the back of a spoon, mash the tarragon into a rough paste. Add the butter and mix thoroughly. Cover and refrigerate.

In the Morning

- Bring the tarragon butter to room temperature. Bring a pan three-fourths full of water to a brisk simmer. With something fine and sharp (a push pin is ideal), pierce the shell at the wide end of each egg, going no more than ¼ inch in. Lower the eggs into the water and cook uncovered, stirring gently once or twice, for 3 to 5 minutes. With a slotted spoon, transfer the eggs to a kitchen towel to drain.
- Serve immediately, using egg cups if desired, or just crack open the eggs and scoop them out of the shells into a small bowl. Top eggs with 1 tablespoon of butter and season with pepper. The remaining butter can be refrigerated for up to 3 days or frozen for up to 1 month.

4 **teaspoons finely chopped fresh tarragon**
Pinch of salt
4 **tablespoons (½ stick) unsalted butter, at room temperature**
2 **eggs**
Freshly ground black pepper

Eggs Coddled with Mushrooms and Sweet Peppers
Serves 4

A college friend of mine spent practically his entire sophomore year dining on coddled eggs cooked up on the hot plate that was the sole kitchen appliance in his rented room. He had an actual coddler—a protective little Victorian-style porcelain cup with a screw-on silver lid, in which an egg and other complementary ingredients of one kind or other were gently simmered in a saucepan of water. Eventually, I think, he acquired more coddlers and began to give dinner parties. Anyway, coddlers are not that common any more, but traditional French porcelain ramekins, topped with foil and surrounded by a hot-water bath, produce equally moist, tender eggs. The method is a good one for entertaining, letting you make individual egg casseroles for any number of people, and the savory foundation upon which they are coddled can be adjusted almost infinitely, to suit your taste, your menu, and the season.

2 tablespoons unsalted butter

⅓ cup finely diced red sweet pepper

2 green onions, thinly sliced

½ pound cultivated white or brown (cremini) mushrooms, wiped clean and finely chopped

½ teaspoon salt

Freshly ground black pepper

4 extra-large eggs

4 teaspoons whipping cream

The Night Before

■ In a skillet over low heat, melt the butter. Add the sweet pepper and onions, cover, and cook, stirring once or twice, for 5 minutes. Add the mushrooms, salt, and ½ teaspoon black pepper, and cook, covered, until the mushrooms begin to render their juices, about 5 minutes. Uncover the skillet, raise the heat, and cook, stirring often, until the juices have evaporated and the vegetables are lightly browned, about 4 minutes. Let cool, cover, and refrigerate.

In the Morning

■ Position a rack in the middle of the oven and preheat to 375 degrees F. Spoon the mushroom mixture into four ½-cup ramekins, dividing it evenly and using it all. Carefully crack an egg into each ramekin. Drizzle each egg with 1 teaspoon of the cream and season with a grinding of black pepper. Cover each ramekin tightly with a square of aluminum foil. Set the ramekins in a shallow baking dish just large enough to hold them. Add hot tap water to the dish to come halfway up the sides of the ramekins. Bake for about 20 minutes, for softly set eggs, or until done to your liking (the eggs will continue to cook for a few minutes after they are removed from the oven).

■ Remove the ramekins from the hot-water bath and pat dry. Remove the foil and serve immediately.

Santa Fe Breakfast Sandwiches

Serves 4

Dee's is a sixties-era Santa Fe coffee shop, scheduled, at this writing, to be razed to make way for a small luxury hotel, which is, in Santa Fe, at least, a very nineties form of "progress." Among Dee's specialties are Dee herself, famed for her quasi-rude repartee; fresh-from-the-fryer homemade donuts; and a breakfast sandwich with "the works," a steamy, greasy, very portable amalgam of eggs, cheese, ham, fiery green chiles, and a prefab hash brown patty, all wrapped in a soft flour tortilla. My version is moister and bigger (also less portable), but otherwise every bit as delicious. Enjoy one as the wrecking ball approaches.

The Night Before

■ In the open flame of a gas burner or under a preheated broiler, roast the chiles, turning them occasionally, until the skins are lightly but evenly charred. Steam the chiles in a closed paper bag until cool. Rub away the burned skin, stem and seed the chiles, and then chop them. There should be about ¾ cup. Cover and refrigerate.

In the Morning

■ Position racks in the upper and lower third of the oven and preheat to 300 degrees F.

■ In a small, heavy, preferably nonstick skillet over medium heat, melt one-fourth of the butter. Crack 2 of the eggs into the hot butter. Cook for 3 minutes, or until partially set. Break the yolks, turn the eggs, and cook until just set but not crisp or dried out, another 2 to 3 minutes. Transfer to a platter. Repeat with the remaining butter and eggs, ending with 4 pairs of eggs in all.

■ In a large, heavy skillet over medium heat, warm a thin layer of the oil. Add the frozen hash brown patties and cook according to the package directions until they are crisp and golden.

■ Meanwhile, lay 2 tortillas on each of 2 baking sheets. Divide the ham among the tortillas, stacking the slices slightly off-center so that they just reach the edge of each tortilla without hanging over. Lay a pair of fried eggs atop each stack of ham slices. Divide the chopped chiles evenly among the eggs, spreading them in a thin layer. Top each pair of eggs with a slice of cheese. Set the baking sheets in the oven and heat just until the cheese is almost melted and the other ingredients are just heated through but the tortillas are not dried out, about 3 minutes.

■ Top each melted cheese slice with a hot hash brown patty. Fold in the sides of a tortilla, then fold up the bottom. Repeat with the remaining sandwiches. Serve immediately.

■■ Note: Long, green Anaheim chiles are widely available but very mild. Fresh New Mexico green chiles are hotter and are preferable here. In some markets in cities with significant Hispanic populations, frozen chopped green chiles, hot or mild, can be found, and will work well here and in other recipes calling for chopped chiles.

4 or 5 long green chiles (see Note)
3 tablespoons unsalted butter
8 eggs
About ½ cup vegetable oil, for the skillet
8 rectangular frozen hash brown patties, such as Ore-Ida brand
4 flour tortillas, each 10 inches in diameter
½ pound baked ham, thinly sliced
4 slices sharp processed cheese, such as Kraft Old English

PANCAKES, WAFFLES, AND FRENCH TOAST

Pumpkin Waffles with Toasted Hazelnut Butter—page 31

Great Buttermilk Pancakes

Makes about ten 4-inch pancakes; serves 3 or 4

Preferring to do things from scratch, but acknowledging that most people think boxed-mix pancakes are wonderful, I resorted to a little detective work (actually I read the label) and learned that Aunt Jemima pancakes include a measure of rice flour. The upshot, since rice flour is gluten free, is a remarkably tender pancake. In my Aunt Jemima knockoff, fresh buttermilk adds tangy flavor, resulting in flapjacks (this is an odd boast) that are actually better than those made from a mix. Here is the formula, followed by several favorite variations. Rice flour can be found in health-food stores.

1¼ cups unbleached all-purpose flour
    (see Note)
¼ cup rice flour, preferably brown
2 tablespoons sugar
1½ teaspoons baking powder
¼ teaspoon salt
2 eggs
3 tablespoons canola or other
    flavorless oil, plus extra oil or
    nonstick spray, for the griddle
1½ cups buttermilk, at room
    temperature
Unsalted butter and warmed maple
    syrup, for serving

- Into a large bowl, sift together twice the all-purpose flour, rice flour, sugar, baking powder, and salt. In a smaller bowl, thoroughly whisk the eggs. Whisk the oil and buttermilk into the eggs. Gradually whisk the egg mixture into the dry ingredients; continue to whisk, just until no lumps remain.
- Position a rack in the middle of the oven and preheat to 250 degrees F.
- Set a large, preferably nonstick griddle or skillet over medium heat, or preheat an electric griddle to 375 degrees F. When it is hot (test by flicking a few drops of water onto the griddle; they should skitter around briefly before evaporating), dip a folded paper towel into the canola oil and lightly brush the griddle. Spoon the batter onto the griddle, allowing 3 tablespoons for each 4-inch pancake. Cook for 1½ to 2 minutes. The pancakes will form a few bubbles on top. Use a spatula to check the undersides of the pancakes; they should be golden brown. Flip the pancakes and cook them until they are just done through, another 1½ minutes. Serve immediately, or keep warm in the oven. Repeat with the remaining batter, lowering the heat under the griddle slightly if necessary to prevent overbrowning, and lightly reoiling as necessary to prevent sticking.
- Serve the pancakes hot with butter and maple syrup.
- ■ Note: To measure the flour, stir it in the canister with a fork to lighten, then spoon into a dry-measure cup and sweep level.

Buckwheat Pancakes

- Use only 1 cup all-purpose flour, and replace the rice flour with ¾ cup buckwheat flour, preferably stone-ground. Prepare the batter and cook as directed above. These are fine indeed with butter and maple syrup, maybe even better with butter and buckwheat honey (available in health-food stores and some gourmet shops).

Grape-nuts Pancakes or Granola Pancakes

- Prepare the basic buttermilk pancake batter, increasing the buttermilk to 1¾ cups. When the batter is smooth, stir in ½ cup Grape-nuts cereal or a basic granola with nuts and dried fruit. Cook as directed, allowing an extra 30 seconds or so cooking time per side. These are especially good with orange honey (available in health-food stores and some gourmet shops).

Bacon-Banana Pancakes

■ Fry 7 slices thick-cut bacon until almost crisp. Drain on paper towels and chop coarsely. Prepare the basic buttermilk pancake batter, substituting 3 tablespoons bacon drippings for the oil. Peel 1 firm but ripe banana and cut it into ¼ inch chunks. Stir the banana and the bacon into the batter. Cook as directed, allowing an extra 30 seconds or so cooking time per side. Serve with butter and maple syrup.

Blueberry Pancakes

■ After the basic buttermilk batter (or buckwheat, Grape-nuts, or granola batter) has been spooned onto the heated griddle, scatter a dozen or so fresh (or still-frozen) blueberries over the pancakes. When the undersides are golden brown, flip the pancakes and cook until done through, another 2 to 3 minutes. Serve these classic pancakes immediately, with the classic accompaniments of butter and maple syrup. Small fresh blackberries can also be used.

Pumpkin Waffles with Toasted Hazelnut Butter

Makes six 6-inch waffles; serves 6

These golden, pumpkiny waffles have a touch of spice, which adds a nice and recognizable holiday flavor, but if you're a real pumpkin lover, you'll enjoy them without the spices as well. The hazelnut butter is delicious and festive (add some panfried turkey sausages and you've got Thanksgiving breakfast), but the waffles are also good—just not as dressed up—with butter and maple syrup. This batter also makes delicious pancakes.

■ Position a rack in the middle of the oven and preheat to 250 degrees F.

■ Into a large bowl, sift together twice the all-purpose flour, sugar, baking powder, cinnamon, ginger, cloves, and salt. In a smaller bowl, thoroughly whisk together room-temperature buttermilk, pumpkin, eggs, and oil. Gradually whisk the pumpkin mixture into the dry ingredients; continue to whisk just until no lumps remain.

■ Heat a waffle iron according to the manufacturer's directions. Coat the iron lightly but evenly with nonstick spray. Spoon about ½ cup batter into the center of the waffle iron (the amount will vary depending upon the waffle iron; the iron should be no more than three-fourths full) and close it. Cook until the waffle is crisp and done through, 3 to 4 minutes.

■ Remove the waffle from the iron (use a fork to pry it gently loose from the iron's grids, if necessary). Serve the waffle immediately, or keep warm in the oven. Repeat with the remaining batter.

■ Serve the waffles hot, accompanied with the hazelnut butter.

■■ Note: To measure the flour, stir it in the canister with a fork to lighten, then spoon into dry-measure cups and sweep level.

1½ **cups unbleached all-purpose flour (see Note)**

2 **tablespoons sugar**

1½ **teaspoon baking powder**

¾ **teaspoon ground cinnamon**

½ **teaspoon ground ginger**

¼ **teaspoon ground cloves**

¼ **teaspoon salt**

1½ **cups buttermilk**

1 **cup unsweetened solid-pack pumpkin purée (not pie filling)**

2 **eggs**

3 **tablespoons canola or other flavorless oil or nonstick spray**

Toasted Hazelnut Butter (page 72)

Atole Pancakes

Makes about ten 4-inch pancakes; serves 3 or 4

Atole is actually a beverage, a thick, cornmeal gruel so nourishing and comforting that at least one hospital in the Southwest prepares it on call, for patients who need special coddling. The name is also applied by a number of regional restaurants to pancakes made of native blue cornmeal. When toasted pine nuts (piñones) are added to the batter, two magnificent local crops are celebrated simultaneously. Maple syrup, definitely not a local crop, is nevertheless the recommended topping.

1 cup plain yogurt, regular or nonfat
½ cup milk
½ teaspoon red wine vinegar
⅓ cup pine nuts (see Note)
1 cup unbleached all-purpose flour (see Note)
¾ cup blue cornmeal
2 tablespoons sugar
1½ teaspoons baking powder
¼ teaspoon salt
2 eggs
3 tablespoons olive oil (see Note)
Canola or other flavorless oil or nonstick spray, for the griddle
Unsalted butter and warmed maple syrup, for serving

- In a bowl, stir together the yogurt, milk, and vinegar. Cover and let stand at room temperature for 30 minutes.
- Meanwhile, position a rack in the middle of the oven and preheat to 375 degrees F. Spread the pine nuts in a metal baking dish (like a pie pan) and set the dish on the rack. Toast the pine nuts, stirring them often, until they are lightly and evenly browned, about 8 minutes. Immediately remove the pan from the oven, transfer the nuts to a dish and let cool completely. Lower the oven temperature to 250 degrees F.
- Into a large bowl, sift together twice the flour, cornmeal, sugar, baking powder, and salt. Whisk the eggs and olive oil into the yogurt mixture. Gradually whisk the yogurt mixture into the dry ingredients; whisk until no lumps remain. Stir in the pine nuts.
- Set a large, preferably nonstick griddle or skillet over medium heat, or preheat an electric griddle to 375 degrees F. When it is hot (test by flicking a few drops of water onto the griddle; they should skitter around briefly before evaporating), dip a folded paper towel into the vegetable oil and lightly brush the griddle. Spoon the batter onto the griddle, allowing 3 tablespoons for each 4-inch pancake. Cook for 1½ to 2 minutes. The pancakes will form a few bubbles on top. Use a spatula to check the undersides of the pancakes; they should be golden brown. Flip the pancakes and cook until they are just done through, another 1½ minutes. Serve immediately, or keep warm in the oven. Repeat with the remaining batter, lowering the heat under the griddle slightly if necessary to prevent overbrowning, and lightly reoiling as necessary to prevent sticking.
- Serve the pancakes hot with butter and maple syrup.
- ■ Note: Because native piñones are difficult to harvest, they are expensive, a situation that has resulted in the importation of large, rather dark, coarse-flavored but inexpensive pine nuts from China. The domestic nuts are preferred, and can be ordered from the Santa Fe School of Cooking and Market Catalog (see Mail-Order Sources).
- To measure the flour, stir it in the canister with a fork to lighten, then spoon into a dry-measure cup and sweep level.
- In robust pancakes like these, the flavor of olive is welcome, not jarring, a suggestion from Elizabeth Alston's *Pancakes and Waffles*. Flavorless vegetable oil can be substituted.

Sand Dollars with Cherry-Amaretto Sauce

Serves 6

These gritty, golden pancake coins, as with all the other flapjacks and waffles in this book, are perfectly delicious served with butter and maple syrup or honey instead of the fancier sauce I have suggested. Either way, for the best texture, use the coarsest, crunchiest stone-ground cornmeal you can locate.

- In a large bowl, thoroughly stir together the flour, cornmeal, sugar, baking powder, and salt. In a smaller bowl, whisk the egg yolks. Whisk in the milk and oil. In a small bowl with a clean whisk, beat the egg whites until soft peaks form. Stir the milk mixture into the dry ingredients. Fold in the egg whites until just combined; do not overmix.
- Position a rack in the middle of the oven and preheat to 250 degrees F.
- Set a large, preferably nonstick griddle or skillet over medium heat, or preheat an electric griddle to 375 degrees F. When it is hot (test by flicking a few drops of water onto the griddle; they should skitter around briefly before evaporating), dip a folded paper towel into the oil and lightly brush the griddle. Spoon the batter onto the griddle, allowing 1 tablespoon for each 2-inch pancake. Cook for about 1 minute. The pancakes will form a few bubbles on top. Use a spatula to check the undersides of the pancakes; they should be golden brown. Flip the pancakes and cook them until they are just done through, about 1 minute longer. Serve immediately, or keep the pancakes warm in the oven. Repeat with the remaining batter, lowering the heat under the griddle slightly if necessary to prevent overbrowning, and lightly reoiling as necessary to prevent sticking.
- Arrange the pancakes on plates. Drizzle with the cherry sauce, sift confectioners' sugar lightly over all, and serve immediately.
- ■ Note: To measure the flour, stir it in the canister with a fork to lighten, then spoon into a dry-measure cup and sweep level.

1 cup unbleached all-purpose flour (see Note)

¾ cup coarse yellow cornmeal or polenta, preferably stone-ground

2 tablespoons sugar

1½ teaspoons baking powder

¼ teaspoon salt

3 eggs, separated

1½ cups milk

3 tablespoons canola or other flavorless oil, plus oil or nonstick spray, for the griddle

Cherry-Amaretto Sauce (page 77), heated to a simmer

Confectioners' sugar, in a sieve

Wild Rice Waffles

Makes six 6-inch waffles; serves 6

Wild rice adds wonderful texture and a nutty flavor to these waffles, while a touch of buckwheat flour contributes muted color and its own special taste. The waffles are great just with butter and maple syrup, or company-wonderful with Toasted Hazelnut Butter (page 72) or Marmalade Butter (page 71).

⅔ cup wild rice, rinsed
Salt
1¼ **cups unbleached all-purpose flour**
    (see Note)
¼ **cup buckwheat flour, preferably**
    stone-ground
2 **tablespoons sugar**
1½ **teaspoons baking powder**
¼ **teaspoon salt**
2 **eggs**
3 **tablespoons olive or corn oil**
1½ **cups buttermilk, at room**
    temperature
Nonstick spray, for the waffle iron
Unsalted butter and warmed maple
    syrup, for serving

The Night Before

■ Bring a saucepan three-fourths full of water to a boil. Stir in the wild rice and 1 teaspoon salt. Cover partially and cook briskly, stirring occasionally, until the rice is just tender and the ends of the kernels are beginning to burst, about 45 minutes. Drain and let cool. Cover and refrigerate.

In the Morning

■ Position a rack in the middle of the oven and preheat to 250 degrees F.

■ Into a large bowl, sift together twice the all-purpose flour, buckwheat flour, sugar, baking powder, and salt. In a smaller bowl, whisk the eggs. Whisk in the oil and buttermilk. Gradually whisk the egg mixture into the dry ingredients; continue to whisk just until no lumps remain. Stir in the wild rice.

■ Heat a waffle iron according to the manufacturer's directions. Coat the iron lightly but evenly with nonstick spray. Spoon about ½ cup batter into the center of the waffle iron (the amount will vary depending upon the waffle iron; the iron should be no more than three-fourths full) and close it. Cook until the waffle is crisp and done through, 3 to 4 minutes.

■ Remove the waffle from the iron (use a fork to pry it gently loose from the iron's grids, if necessary). Serve the waffle immediately, or keep warm in the oven. Repeat with the remaining batter.

■ Serve the waffles hot, accompanied with butter and maple syrup.

■■ Note: To measure the flour, stir it in the canister with a fork to lighten, then spoon into dry-measure cups and sweep level.

Cheddar-Corn Waffles with Pepper Jelly Syrup

Makes six 8-inch waffles; serves 6

Despite the gutsy-sounding list of ingredients, these are breakfast waffles. Although they will surely be an adventure to some, my southwestern tasters found them perfect morning fare, and I think most open-minded diners will agree. Accompany them with Oven-Glazed Pepper Bacon (page 44) and, if you like, top each waffle with a fried egg.

- Position a rack in the middle of the oven and preheat to 250 degrees F.
- Into a large bowl, sift together twice the flour, cornmeal, sugar, paprika, baking powder, and salt. In a smaller bowl, whisk together the eggs and oil. Whisk in the buttermilk. Gradually whisk the egg mixture into the dry ingredients; continue to whisk just until no lumps remain. Stir in the corn and cheese.
- Heat a waffle iron according to the manufacturer's directions. Coat the iron lightly but evenly with nonstick spray. Spoon about ½ cup batter into the center of the waffle iron (the amount will vary depending upon the waffle iron; the iron should be no more than three-fourths full) and close it. Cook until the waffle is crisp, golden, and done through, about 4 minutes.
- Remove the waffle from the iron (use a fork to pry it gently loose from the iron's grids, if necessary). Serve the waffle immediately, or keep it warm in the oven. Repeat with the remaining batter.
- Spoon 3 or 4 tablespoons of the heated syrup over each waffle and serve hot.
- ■ Note: To measure the flour, stir it in the canister with a fork to lighten, then spoon into a dry-measure cup and sweep level.

1 cup unbleached all-purpose flour (see Note)

¾ cup coarse yellow cornmeal, preferably stone-ground

2 tablespoons sugar

2 tablespoons Hungarian sweet paprika

1½ teaspoons baking powder

¼ teaspoon salt

2 eggs

⅓ cup canola or other flavorless oil

1½ cups buttermilk, at room temperature

1 cup corn kernels (canned or thawed, frozen), well drained

¼ pound sharp Cheddar cheese, shredded (about 1 cup)

Nonstick spray, for the waffle iron

Amy's Pepper Jelly Syrup (page 71), heated to a simmer

Praline Apple Pain Perdu

Serves 8

In New Orleans, *pain perdu* is "lost bread," which, although day old, is not lost at all. Rather it is frugally transformed into thick slices of batter-soaked baguette, fried, and then topped, in this version, with a sauté of caramelized apples and pecans. Eggs any fashion and thick-cut bacon are fine accompaniments, although one hedonistic friend of mine recommends a scoop of premium vanilla ice cream.

9 **eggs, beaten**

2¼ **cups milk**

¼ **cup plus 2 tablespoons orange liqueur**

1½ **tablespoons vanilla extract**

1½ **teaspoons ground cinnamon**

1 **pound (1 or 2 loaves) day-old crusty baguette, preferably semolina (see Note), sliced on the diagonal into sixteen 1-inch-thick pieces**

7 **tablespoons unsalted butter**

3 **Granny Smith or other tart cooking apples, (about 1½ pounds), peeled, cored, and cut into ½-inch chunks**

1½ **cups (about 6 ounces) coarsely chopped pecans**

⅔ **cup packed light brown sugar**

1 **cup hot water**

Canola or other flavorless oil or nonstick spray, for the griddle

- In a bowl, thoroughly whisk the eggs. Stir in the milk, orange liqueur, vanilla, and cinnamon. Arrange the bread slices in a single layer in a shallow dish just large enough to hold them. Pour the egg mixture over the bread slices. Let stand at room temperature, turning once or twice, until the bread slices have absorbed all the egg mixture, about 20 minutes.
- Position a rack in the middle of the oven and preheat to 250 degrees F.
- In a large, heavy skillet over medium heat, melt the butter. Add the apples and cook uncovered, stirring once or twice, for 5 minutes. Lower the heat slightly, add the pecans and cook, stirring once or twice, for 5 minutes. Stir in the brown sugar and the 1 cup hot water and cook, stirring constantly, until the mixture thickens, about 3 minutes. Remove from the heat and keep warm.
- Set a large, preferably nonstick griddle or skillet over medium heat, or preheat an electric griddle to 375 degrees F. When it is hot (test by flicking a few drops of water onto the griddle; they should skitter around briefly before evaporating), dip a folded paper towel into the oil and lightly brush the griddle. Working in batches, add the bread to the skillet and cook until crisp and brown on both sides, about 6 minutes' total cooking time. Lower the temperature under the griddle slightly to prevent overbrowning. Reoil the griddle as needed to prevent sticking. Serve the *pain perdu* immediately, or keep the bread slices warm in the oven until all are fried.
- Arrange 2 slices of bread on each of 8 plates. Spoon the apple mixture over the bread, dividing it evenly and using it all. Serve immediately.
- ■ Note: The firm-textured golden bread made from semolina flour (the same flour used in good-quality pastas) is ideal for soaking up the maximum amount of batter without falling apart. Substitute any similar firm bread that, when diagonally cut, produces a slice about 2 inches by 4 inches.

PB & J French Toast Sandwiches

Serves 4

Sleepy little people (of all ages) will like these breakfast sandwiches, for which the PB and the J are spread between two slices of good bread, dipped into an eggy, vanilla-scented batter, and then panfried. Traditionalists will insist on grape jelly; adventurers might consider raspberry jam, orange marmalade, or apple butter. Both schools are free to use smooth or chunky peanut butter, or even cashew butter. Ham, bacon, or sausage will provide a pleasantly salty relief to this sweet treat.

- Position a rack in the middle of the oven and preheat to 250 degrees F.
- In a shallow bowl, thoroughly whisk together the milk, eggs, sugar, and vanilla.
- Spread 1 side of each of 4 slices of the bread with a thin, even layer of peanut butter that entirely covers the side. Spread the peanut butter with a thin, even layer of the jelly that entirely covers the peanut butter. Set the remaining 4 slices of bread atop the jelly.
- Working in batches if necessary, soak the sandwiches in the milk mixture, turning them carefully once, until very wet.
- Set a large, preferably nonstick griddle or skillet over medium heat, or preheat an electric griddle to 375 degrees F. When it is hot (test by flicking a few drops of water onto the griddle; they should skitter around briefly before evaporating), dip a folded paper towel into the oil and lightly brush the griddle. Working in batches if necessary, carefully add the soaked sandwiches and cook them, moving them around on the griddle to promote even browning and turning them once at the halfway point, until they are crisp and golden on both sides, 9 to 10 minutes' total cooking time.
- Serve the sandwiches immediately, or keep warm in the oven. Repeat with the remaining sandwiches.
- Drizzle with maple syrup or sprinkle with confectioners' sugar and serve hot.

1½ cups milk
6 eggs, beaten
3 tablespoons sugar
1 tablespoon vanilla extract
8 slices firm home-style white bread, each ½ inch thick
About ¼ cup peanut butter
About ¼ cup jelly or preserves of choice
Canola or other flavorless oil or nonstick spray, for the griddle
Warmed maple syrup or confectioners' sugar (in a sieve), for serving

French Toast Fingers with Marmalade Butter

Serves 4 to 6

Cutting the bread for French toast into sticks, or "fingers," increases the labor intensiveness of things somewhat, but it so much fun to eat them (ideally, with the fingers) that I make the time, especially if there are children or immature adults in the house. Marmalade butter is perfectly delicious here (spreading it onto each bite as you go is part of the ritual), but so too is maple syrup, offered in small bowls for dipping.

- In a bowl, thoroughly whisk the eggs. Whisk in the milk, sugar, and vanilla. Working in batches, add some of the bread fingers to the egg mixture and let stand until they are well saturated but not falling apart.
- Position a rack in the middle of the oven and preheat to 250 degrees F.
- Set a large, preferably nonstick griddle or skillet over medium heat, or preheat an electric skillet to 375 degrees F. When it is hot (test by flicking a few drops of water onto the griddle; they should skitter around briefly before evaporating), dip a folded paper towel into the oil and lightly brush the griddle.
- Working in batches if necessary, carefully transfer the soaked bread fingers to the griddle and cook, turning, until golden brown, about 1 minute per side. Serve immediately, or keep warm in the oven. Repeat with the remaining ingredients.
- Transfer the fingers to plates, sieve confectioners' sugar lightly over them, and serve hot, accompanied with the butter.

4 **eggs**
1 **cup milk**
2 **tablespoons sugar**
2 **teaspoons vanilla extract**
12 **slices firm home-style white bread, each ¼ inch thick, crusts trimmed, and each slice cut lengthwise into rectangular fingers**
Canola or other flavorless oil or nonstick spray, for the griddle
Confectioners' sugar, in a sieve
Marmalade Butter (page 71), softened slightly

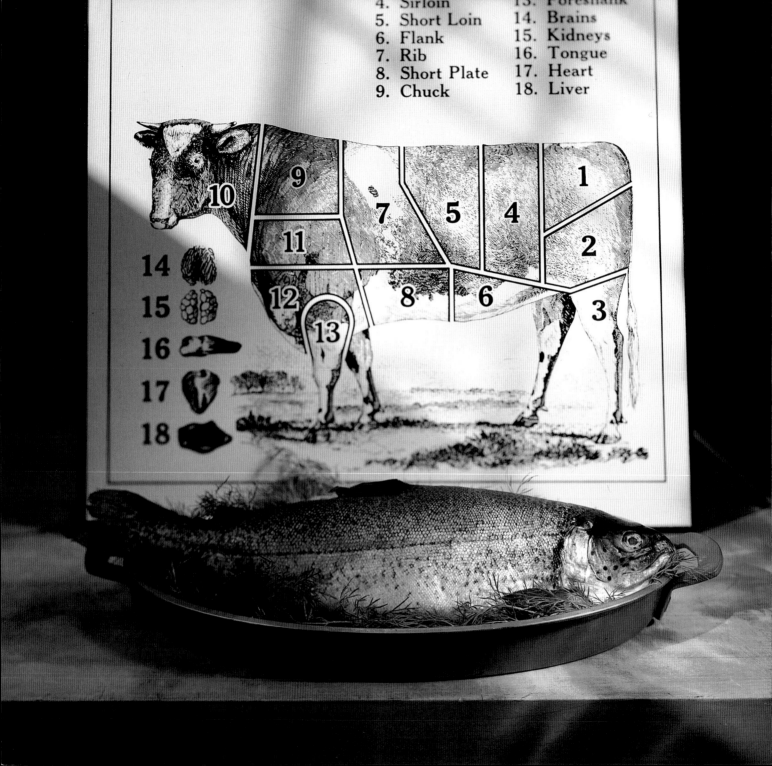

MEATS AND FISH

Corned Beef Hash Boats with Poached Eggs

Serves 4

Baking canned hash—corned or roast beef—in hollowed-out potatoes has a kind of friendly fifties air about it. Morning is probably the best time for such funky festivity, mild novelty—but not actual eccentricity—being as good a way to ease into the day as any. If poaching eggs is too much trouble too early, offer scrambled eggs on the side instead. A fifty-fifty mixture of hot salsa and ketchup is a fine condiment for the hash.

4 russet (baking) potatoes, 10 ounces each, well scrubbed

2 tablespoons solid vegetable shortening or corn oil

1 can (16 ounces) corned beef or roast beef hash

½ cup prepared hot salsa

½ cup ketchup

4 poached eggs (page 24)

The Night Before

- Position a rack in the middle of the oven and preheat to 400 degrees F.
- Rub the unpeeled potatoes well with the shortening. With a fork, prick the top of each potato once or twice. Set the potatoes directly on the oven rack and bake until just tender, about 1 hour.
- Transfer the potatoes to a cooling rack and let stand until just cool enough to handle. With a small knife, cut a generous oval opening (large enough to hold a poached egg) in the upper peel of each potato. With a spoon, scoop out the oval piece of peel and the insides of the potato, leaving a shell about ¼ inch thick. Cool the potato shells completely, then wrap well and refrigerate.

In the Morning

- Position a rack in the middle of the oven and preheat to 350 degrees F.
- Set the potato shells on a baking sheet. Spoon the hash into the potato shells, dividing it evenly, using it all, and creating a slight depression in the top with the back of a spoon. Bake until the potato shells are crisp and the hash is hot and lightly browned, about 30 minutes.
- Meanwhile, in a small bowl stir together the salsa and ketchup. When the hash boats are ready, place a boat on each of 4 plates. Set a poached egg atop each boat. Serve immediately, accompanied with the salsa ketchup.

Scrambled Eggs with Smoked Trout and Broiled Tomatoes

Serves 8

This relatively simple dish of eggs scrambled with chives, topped with chunks of moist trout, and garnished with broiled tomato halves illustrates one morning advantage of high-quality smoked meats and fish: Most of the work has been done by the smokehouse, and the cook needs only to provide a sensibly simple setting to show them off. People are always sending me smoked things around the holidays, and these eggs, accompanied by sausages or rashers of bacon and toast with marmalade, make an ideal British-style Christmas-morning breakfast. Six ounces of smoked salmon, cut into small pieces, can be substituted for the trout.

- Position a rack about 6 inches from the broiler and preheat. Arrange the tomatoes, cut sides up, on a baking sheet. Broil until lightly colored and tender, watching closely to avoid burning, about 5 minutes. Remove from the broiler, season to taste with salt and pepper, and tent with aluminum foil to keep warm.
- In a large bowl, whisk the eggs with a few swift strokes of a fork. Add the cream, 1¼ teaspoons salt, and ¾ teaspoon pepper and whisk again.
- In a large, heavy skillet over medium heat, melt the butter. Add the eggs and cook, stirring occasionally, until almost set, about 6 minutes. Stir in the chives and remove from the heat.
- Spoon the eggs onto plates. Scatter the smoked trout over the eggs. Set the tomatoes next to the eggs and serve immediately.

4 tomatoes, halved crosswise
Salt
Freshly ground black pepper
12 eggs
⅓ cup whipping cream
4 tablespoons (½ stick) unsalted butter
2 tablespoons minced fresh chives
1 pound (2 medium) smoked trout, skinned, boned, and flaked

Campfire Trout with Hazelnut Sauce
Serves 4

Farmed trout are so widely available (and I'm so lazy), that I developed this method for re-creating the incredible, slightly smoky flavor of just-caught fish cooked over an open fire. A little of the outdoor magic may be missing (so will the joy of sleeping on cold, hard ground), but all the good eating remains intact, since the creamy hazelnut pan sauce picks up just the right touch of smoke.

- If using a charcoal grill or a gas grill with lava rocks, soak the wood chips in water to cover for at least 30 minutes.
- In a pie plate, stir together the flour, ¾ teaspoon salt, and ½ teaspoon pepper.
- Light a charcoal fire and let it burn down until the coals are evenly white, or preheat a gas grill (medium-high). Drain the wood chips if you have soaked them and scatter them over the coals or firestones around the edges of the grill (or follow the manufacturer's directions for using unsoaked chips in a grill with a smoking compartment).
- Dredge the trout in the seasoned flour; shake off the excess. Position the rack about 6 inches above the heat source. When the chips are smoking heavily, set a large, heavy nonreactive skillet on the grill rack. Melt 4 tablespoons of the butter in the skillet. When it foams, add the trout. Cover the grill and cook for 4 minutes. With a long, wide spatula, carefully turn the trout. Cover the grill and cook until done but still moist, another 3 to 4 minutes. Transfer to plates and keep warm.
- Wipe out the skillet. Add the remaining 3 tablespoons butter to the skillet and set on the grill. Add the hazelnuts and cook, stirring, until golden, 1 to 2 minutes. Stir in the green onions and cook for 30 seconds. Remove the skillet from the heat and stir in the crème fraîche, lemon juice, ½ teaspoon salt, and ¼ teaspoon pepper. Spoon the sauce over the trout and serve.

3 cups wood chips, preferably hickory or apple
½ cup unbleached all-purpose flour
Salt
Freshly ground black pepper
4 medium trout, about 3 pounds total, cleaned and scaled
7 tablespoons unsalted butter
½ cup coarsely chopped hazelnuts
⅓ cup thinly sliced green onions
¾ cup crème fraîche or whipping cream
2 tablespoons fresh lemon juice

Oven-Glazed Pepper Bacon

Serves 6 to 8

The notion of lightly sugared bacon, oven-baked until crisp, is not a new one; it turns up in Junior League cookbooks all the time. My touches of brown sugar and plenty of fresh black pepper are not typical, though, and the result—salty, sweetly smoky, and just slightly fiery—usually has people who "never" eat bacon fighting for the last sticky piece on the platter.

1½ pounds (about 18 strips) thick-sliced bacon
Freshly ground black pepper
½ cup packed light brown sugar

- Position racks in the upper and lower thirds of the oven and preheat to 350 degrees F. Line 2 jelly roll pans with aluminum foil.
- For easier handling, bring the bacon to room temperature. Separate the strips and arrange them, without overlapping, on the prepared pans. Grind fresh pepper generously over the bacon strips. Sprinkle the brown sugar evenly over the bacon strips, using it all.
- Set the pans in the oven. Bake without turning the strips, pouring off any rendered drippings and exchanging the positions of the pans on the racks from top to bottom and from front to back at the halfway point, until the bacon is browned and almost, but not quite, crisp, about 25 minutes. Immediately transfer the bacon with tongs to a heated platter. Serve hot.

Sausage-Stuffed Baked Apples with Maple-Marmalade Glaze

Serves 4

Here's another stuffed breakfast main dish, homey if not downright retro. The apples make a nice buffet dish, or just serve them plated, with eggs and toast alongside. Don't go looking for fancy sausage to use here; good old Jimmy Dean works just fine.

½ cup orange marmalade
½ cup water
2 tablespoons maple syrup
4 Granny Smith or other tart cooking apples, about 2 pounds total
¾ pound bulk sage or spicy breakfast sausage
Freshly ground black pepper

- Position a rack in the middle of the oven and preheat to 350 degrees F.
- In a shallow baking dish just large enough to hold the apples comfortably, stir together the marmalade, water, and maple syrup.
- Completely core the apples through their bottoms, enlarging the resulting openings until they are about 1 inch in diameter. Stuff the sausage into the openings, dividing it evenly, using it all, and mounding it slightly atop the apples. Set the apples in the shallow baking dish.
- Set the dish in the oven and bake for 10 minutes. Baste the apples with the marmalade mixture and continue to bake, basting every 10 minutes, until the visible sausage is browned, the apples are just tender when pierced with a knife, and the glaze has thickened, about 40 minutes' total cooking time.
- Remove from the oven and let the apples rest in the dish on a rack, basting them once or twice, for 5 minutes. Serve hot, drizzling the apples with any glaze remaining in the pan.

Double Salmon Cakes—page 46
Double-Hominy Grits with Cheese and Green Onions—page 58

Double Salmon Cakes

Serves 4

Salmon cakes for breakfast are likely to turn up in soul-food restaurants, most of the time made from canned salmon. There's nothing wrong with that (it's probably the best thing to do with canned salmon), but when made with freshly poached fish, the ordinary becomes fairly sublime. These cakes are studded with bits of smoked salmon—use either the moist, translucent Scottish type or the drier hot smoke–cured Alaskan sort. Team them with fried eggs, Spicy Peach Ketchup (page 76), the cheese grits on page 58, and Peppered Buttermilk Biscuits (page 51).

1½ **pounds (3 medium) salmon steaks**
  2 **tablespoons red wine vinegar**
Salt
½ **cup finely crushed saltine crackers**
  2 **eggs, beaten**
⅓ **cup minced yellow onion**
  2 **ounces smoked salmon, finely**
     chopped
¼ **cup minced celery**
  3 **tablespoons mayonnaise**
  2 **teaspoons prepared mustard**
¾ **teaspoon freshly ground black**
     pepper
  2 **tablespoons bacon drippings or**
     vegetable oil
Lemon wedges, for serving

The Night Before

■ In a large, deep skillet, combine the salmon steaks with enough water just to cover. Add the vinegar and 1 teaspoon salt and set the skillet over medium heat. Bring to a gentle simmer, then cook the salmon steaks, turning them once, until they are just beginning to flake, about 8 minutes. Remove the skillet from the heat and cool the salmon steaks to room temperature in the poaching liquid.

■ Remove the steaks from the poaching liquid and pat dry. Remove the skin and bones and coarsely flake the fish into a bowl. Add the crushed crackers, eggs, onion, smoked salmon, celery, mayonnaise, mustard, pepper, and ½ teaspoon salt and mix lightly but thoroughly. Shape the salmon mixture into 4 thick patties and transfer to a plate. Wrap well and refrigerate.

In the Morning

■ In a large, heavy preferably nonstick skillet over medium heat, warm the bacon drippings. Add the salmon patties and cook, turning once, until crisp and brown, about 8 minutes' total cooking time. Serve immediately.

Fund-Raiser's Creamed Chipped Beef

Serves 4

The general notion of a fancified S.O.S. came from a Pennsylvania woman, who explained to me that it was the most popular item on her unspecified group's fund-raising breakfast menu. (Obviously it wasn't the VFW Auxiliary.) The addition of colorful vegetables does add flavor and somewhat lighten the dish, one I grew up eating and loving. It's good spooned over toast or English muffins, even better over Peppered Buttermilk Biscuits (page 51) or Creamed Hash Browns (page 60).

- Separate the slices of meat. In a sieve under warm running water, briefly rinse the slices. Drain well and cut into ¼-inch-wide strips.
- In a large skillet over low heat, melt the bacon drippings. Add the peppers, onions, and garlic; cover and cook, stirring once or twice, until almost tender, about 8 minutes. Sprinkle the flour over the vegetables and cook, stirring often without browning the flour, for 2 minutes. Gradually whisk in the milk. Stir in the Worcestershire sauce, ¾ teaspoon salt, and the pepper and bring to a simmer. Cook uncovered, stirring occasionally, until the gravy begins to thicken, about 5 minutes.
- Add the meat strips and cook, stirring often, until the gravy is very thick, another 2 to 3 minutes. Adjust the seasoning. Serve hot.

I jar (4½ ounces) dried sliced beef
3 tablespoons bacon drippings or butter
I cup finely diced sweet red peppers
½ cup thinly sliced green onions
I garlic clove, minced
3 tablespoons unbleached all-purpose flour
3 cups milk
2 teaspoons Worcestershire sauce
Salt
I teaspoon freshly ground black pepper

Chicken Livers in Peppery Gravy

Serves 2 to 4

These panfried livers, finished in a well-peppered milk gravy, should be served over toast, biscuits, or some other sauce-absorbent starch, and can be accompanied by eggs. The recipe will feed two liver lovers or four regular carnivores, especially if a strip or two of bacon or a slice of ham is added, ranch style, to the already well-filled plates.

- Position a rack in the middle of the oven and preheat to 250 degrees F.
- On a plate, stir together the flour, ½ teaspoon salt, and ½ teaspoon pepper.
- In a large, preferably nonstick skillet over medium-high heat, warm the oil. Dredge the livers in the seasoned flour. Reserve 2 tablespoons of the flour. When the oil is hot, add the livers and cook, turning once, until lightly colored outside but still pinkish red inside, about 4 minutes. With a slotted spoon, transfer the livers to a plate and set them in the oven to keep them warm.
- Lower the heat under the skillet. Whisk the reserved 2 tablespoons flour into the pan drippings and cook, stirring often, for I minute. Whisk in the milk. Stir in ½ teaspoon salt and additional black pepper, up to I teaspoon, or to taste. Bring the gravy to a simmer and cook uncovered, stirring often, until the gravy begins to thicken, about 5 minutes.
- Return the livers to the skillet and simmer them in the gravy, stirring gently, until they are just cooked through while remaining moist and the gravy is thick, about 2 minutes. Adjust the seasoning and serve immediately.

½ cup unbleached all-purpose flour
Salt
Freshly ground black pepper
3 tablespoons canola or other flavorless oil
I pound chicken livers, trimmed, halved, and patted thoroughly dry
2 cups milk

BREADS, SWEET ROLLS, MUFFINS, AND BISCUITS

5

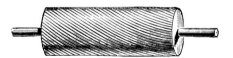

Cinnamon, Date, and Walnut Toasting Bread

Makes two 8-by-4-inch loaves

This firm, easily sliced loaf, with its internal spiral of cinnamon, nuts, and dates, was intended to make wonderful toast, and so it does (especially good with bitter English marmalade). It freezes well, too, so you can keep the spare loaf on hand for such emergency nonbreakfast uses as ham-and-cheese sandwiches or bread pudding.

2 cups milk

2 tablespoons unsalted butter, plus room-temperature butter for the bread pans

4 teaspoons sugar

1 tablespoon salt

1 package (2½ teaspoons) active dry yeast

About 5 cups unbleached all-purpose flour

1 tablespoon canola or other flavorless oil

1½ teaspoons ground cinnamon

1½ cups chopped pitted dates

1½ cups coarsely chopped walnuts

■ In a small saucepan over low heat, combine the milk, butter, sugar, and salt. Heat, stirring, until the butter just melts. Transfer the milk mixture to a large bowl. When the temperature of the milk has fallen to between 105 and 115 degrees F, sprinkle the yeast over the milk. Stir to dissolve and let stand until foamy, about 5 minutes. Stir in about 4 cups of the flour, ½ cup at a time, to form a soft, sticky dough.

■ Flour a work surface. Turn out the dough and knead, adding more flour as necessary, until it is soft, smooth, and elastic, about 5 minutes. Coat a large bowl with the oil. Add the dough, turn it to coat it with the oil, and cover the bowl with a clean towel. Let rise at room temperature until doubled, about 2 hours.

■ Butter two 8-by-4-inch loaf pans, preferably of metal. Lightly flour a work surface. Punch down the dough, turn it out, and divide it in half. Pat and roll one-half out into an 8-by-14-inch rectangle. Sprinkle half the cinnamon evenly over the rectangle. Scatter half the dates and half the walnuts evenly over the rectangle. Starting from a short side, roll up the dough to form a loaf and transfer to a prepared pan. Repeat with the remaining dough, cinnamon, dates, and walnuts. Cover the pans with a towel and let rise at room temperature until doubled, about 1½ hours.

■ Position a rack in the middle of the oven and preheat to 400 degrees F. Bake the loaves until they are fully risen, golden brown, and sound hollow when thumped on the bottom, about 30 minutes. Remove the loaves from the pans and let them cool to room temperature on a rack before slicing.

Peppered Buttermilk Biscuits

Makes up to 13 medium biscuits

Biscuits from a mix (or, heaven forbid, a refrigerated tube) are not much more than starchy fodder, something to butter and get on with. By contrast, homemade biscuits, flaky, tender, and in this case, spiked with plenty of freshly ground black pepper, are another thing altogether, and will earn as much diners' respect as whatever wonderful stuff is in the center of the plate.

- Position a rack in the middle of the oven and preheat to 450 degrees F.
- Into a large bowl, sift together twice the all-purpose flour, cake flour, baking powder, sugar, pepper, and salt. With a pastry blender, cut the vegetable shortening and butter into the dry ingredients until bits the size of corn kernels form. With as few strokes as possible, stir in the buttermilk to form a soft, crumbly dough. Lightly flour a work surface.
- Turn out the dough, gather it together, and knead it briefly, until it just holds together. Roll out the dough ½ inch thick. Using a sharp round biscuit cutter 3 inches in diameter, cut out 8 or 9 biscuits, transferring them as you do so to an ungreased baking sheet. Gather the remaining dough into a ball (do not overhandle; do not add additional flour to the work surface unless absolutely necessary to prevent sticking), roll it out ½ inch thick, and cut out 3 or 4 more biscuits. Transfer them to the baking sheet.
- Bake the biscuits until they are puffed, the tops and bottoms are golden brown, and the centers are fully cooked through although still fluffy and moist, about 12 minutes. Serve immediately.
- ■ Note: To measure the flour, stir it in the canister with a fork to lighten, then spoon into dry-measure cups and sweep level.

2¾ cups unbleached all-purpose flour (see Note), plus flour for the work surface

1 cup cake flour, not self-rising (see Note)

2 tablespoons baking powder

1 tablespoon sugar

2 teaspoons freshly ground black pepper

1 teaspoon salt

⅔ cup solid vegetable shortening, well chilled, cut into pieces

4 tablespoons (½ stick) chilled unsalted butter, cut into pieces

1½ cups chilled buttermilk

Maple-Glazed Cinnamon Rolls
Makes 12

My grandmother Hazel was a fine farm-trained baker, always at her best with morning sweets and treats. Her standard breakfast menu (originally designed to fortify field hands against a ten- or twelve-hour day) typically included eggs, bacon, and/or sausage, potatoes, and toasted homemade bread, along with peach butter, applesauce, and stewed rhubarb—options enough for even the hungriest early riser. Still, no breakfast was complete without some kind of sweet pastry, cinnamon rolls as likely as not, warm and puffy from the oven. I remember them as enormous (I was smaller then), and so this recipe makes BIG rolls, substantial enough that modern urban appetites might consider them breakfast on their own.

Rolls

1½ cups milk

12 tablespoons (1½ sticks) unsalted butter, plus room-temperature butter for the bowl and the baking dish

2 tablespoons plus ⅓ cup sugar

¾ teaspoon salt

2 teaspoons active dry yeast

2 eggs, beaten

About 4½ cups unbleached all-purpose flour

2 teaspoons ground cinnamon

Glaze

6 tablespoons genuine maple syrup

2 tablespoons whipping cream

1 tablespoon unsalted butter

1 teaspoon vanilla extract

2 cups confectioners' sugar, in a sieve

2 to 3 tablespoons dried cranberries, pitted dried cherries, or dark raisins

2 to 3 tablespoons sliced unblanched almonds

The Night Before

■ For the rolls, in a saucepan over medium heat, combine the milk, 6 tablespoons of the butter, the 2 tablespoons sugar, and the salt. Heat, stirring once or twice, until the milk is hot and the butter is just melted. Remove from the heat and pour into a large bowl.

■ When the temperature of the milk has fallen to between 105 and 115 degrees F, sprinkle the yeast over the milk. Stir to dissolve and let stand until foamy, about 5 minutes. Stir in the beaten eggs. Stir in about 4 cups of the flour, ½ cup at a time, to form a soft, sticky dough.

■ Flour a work surface. Turn out the dough and knead, adding additional flour as needed, until it is smooth and elastic, about 5 minutes. Butter a large bowl. Put the dough in the bowl, turn it to coat with the butter, and cover with a clean towel. Let rise at room temperature until doubled, about 2 hours. Punch down the dough. Knead it briefly in the bowl, then cover the bowl with plastic wrap and refrigerate overnight.

In the Morning

■ Let the remaining 6 tablespoons butter come to room temperature.

■ Turn out the chilled dough onto a lightly floured work surface. Pat and roll it out into an 11-by-15inch rectangle about ⅓ inch thick. In a small bowl, stir together the ⅓ cup sugar and the cinnamon. Spread the 6 tablespoons softened butter evenly over the dough to the edges. Sprinkle the cinnamon-sugar mixture evenly over the buttered dough. Starting from a long side, roll up the dough into a long cylinder. Cut the cylinder crosswise into 12 equal slices. Butter a 9-by-13-inch baking dish. Arrange the 12 dough slices cut sides down, in the dish in 3 rows of 4 slices. Cover the dish with a clean towel and let the rolls rise at room temperature until they are doubled, about 2 hours.

■ Position a rack in the middle of the oven and preheat to 350 degrees F.

■ Set the dish in the oven and bake the rolls until they are puffed, golden, and cooked through, about 30 minutes. Remove from the oven and let stand in the dish on a rack for 15 minutes. Transfer to a serving platter.

- Meanwhile, in the top pan of a double boiler over simmering water, stir together the maple syrup, cream, butter, and vanilla. Gradually sift in the confectioners' sugar, stirring constantly. Remove the glaze from the hot water and let cool slightly.
- When the glaze has thickened slightly from cooling, drizzle it evenly over the warm rolls, using it all. Sprinkle the glaze evenly with the cranberries and almonds. Serve warm.

Cranberry-Buttermilk Scones
Makes 12

Biscuit tender and flecked with tangy red cranberry bits, these scones are best served hot from the oven, with plenty of Orange Curd (page 73) or sweet butter and tart orange marmalade. Like all such quick breads, they stir together with minimal fuss, and with repeated practice you may not even need to be awake. Dried pitted cherries, dried blueberries, or dried currants can be substituted for the cranberries.

- Position a rack in the middle of the oven and preheat to 375 degrees F. Butter two 9-inch round cake pans.
- In a small bowl, whisk 2 of the eggs. Whisk in the buttermilk. Into a large bowl, sift together the flour, the ¼ cup sugar, baking powder, and salt. With a pastry blender, cut the 10 tablespoons chilled butter into the flour mixture until pieces the size of peas form. Add the buttermilk mixture and the cranberries and stir until just combined; the dough will be crumbly. Lightly flour a work surface.
- Turn the dough out and knead it 10 or 12 times, just until a soft dough forms. Divide the dough in half and shape each half into a ball. Roll each ball out into an 8-inch round about 1 inch thick. Carefully transfer each round to one of the prepared pans. With a pizza wheel or a sharp knife, score each dough round into 8 wedges. In a small bowl, whisk the remaining egg with the water. Brush the glaze evenly and generously over the scones.
- Sprinkle evenly with the 2 teaspoons sugar.
- Bake until the scones are puffed and golden and the edges are crisp and lightly browned, 25 to 30 minutes. Remove from the oven and cool the scones in the pans on a rack for 5 minutes. Cut the scones into wedges along the score marks. Serve hot.
- ■ Note: To measure the flour, stir it in the canister with a fork to lighten, then spoon into a dry-measure cup and sweep level.

Room-temperature unsalted butter for the baking pans, plus 10 tablespoons (1¼ sticks) chilled unsalted butter, cut into small pieces

3 eggs

½ cup chilled buttermilk

3 cups unbleached all-purpose flour (see Note), plus flour for the work surface

¼ cup plus 2 teaspoons sugar

1¾ teaspoons baking powder

¼ teaspoon salt

¾ cup sweetened dried cranberries

1 teaspoon water

Carrot-Currant Bran Muffins

Makes 12 muffins

Packed with fiber and various other good nutritional things, these muffins nevertheless taste terrific. Serve them spread with plenty of sweet cream butter, apple butter, or both.

2 cups unprocessed wheat bran

1½ cups whole-wheat flour, preferably stoneground

1 teaspoon baking powder

1 teaspoon ground cinnamon

¾ teaspoon salt

⅔ cup packed light brown sugar

⅔ cup corn oil

2 eggs

1 cup buttermilk, at room temperature

1½ cups coarsely shredded carrots

⅔ cup dried currants

Nonstick spray, for the muffin tin

■ Position a rack in the middle of the oven and preheat to 400 degrees F.

■ In a medium bowl, thoroughly stir together the bran, flour, baking powder, cinnamon, and salt. In a large bowl, whisk together the brown sugar, oil, and eggs. Whisk in the buttermilk. Stir in the dry ingredients. Add the carrots and currants and stir until just combined. Spray the cups of a standard muffin tin well with nonstick spray. Spoon the batter into the prepared cups, dividing it evenly.

■ Bake the muffins until they are puffed and browned, and a tester, inserted into the center of a muffin, comes out clean, about 25 minutes. Remove from the oven and cool the muffins in the tin on a rack for 5 minutes. Turn them out of the tin and let cool further. The muffins are best served warm or at room temperature, not hot.

Whole-Wheat Quesadillas

Serves 2 to 4

Quesadillas—cheese sandwiched between two tortillas and griddled until melted—make fine cocktail munches. They're also good in the morning, however, especially when made with the small, thick whole-wheat tortillas popular in northern New Mexico. Cut them into quarters after they're crisp and gooey, and serve two pieces alongside a substantial southwestern breakfast, or four pieces to accompany simple eggs of some kind.

Nonstick spray

4 whole-wheat tortillas, each 6 inches in diameter

6 ounces jalapeño jack cheese, thinly sliced

⅓ cup thinly sliced green onions

■ Lightly coat a large skillet with nonstick spray and set it over medium heat. Lay 1 tortilla in the skillet. Arrange half the cheese evenly over the tortilla and sprinkle the cheese with half the green onions. Set a second tortilla atop the cheese. Weight the quesadilla with a small plate and cook until the cheese is beginning to melt and the bottom tortilla is lightly browned, about 1½ minutes. Remove the plate. Coat the top tortilla lightly with nonstick spray. Flip the quesadilla, weight it again, and cook until the bottom tortilla is lightly browned and the cheese is melted, another minute or so.

■ Transfer to a cutting board, cut into wedges, and serve immediately. Repeat with the remaining ingredients.

ESSENTIAL STARCHES

6

Oven-Crisped New Potatoes

Serves 4

This remarkably simple recipe produces spuds that are crisp-golden on the outside, creamily tender within and always has people asking what the secret is. There isn't one really, although I do think that these potatoes are especially delicious when made with the bacon drippings.

1½ pounds (about 10) red-skinned new potatoes, well scrubbed and quartered

3 tablespoons rendered bacon drippings, olive oil, or corn oil

¼ teaspoon salt

3 tablespoons minced fresh flat-leaf parsley or chives (optional)

Freshly ground black pepper

- Position a rack in the middle of the oven and preheat to 400 degrees F.
- In a shallow baking dish that will hold the potatoes more or less in a single layer, toss the potatoes together with the bacon drippings. Set the dish in the oven and bake, stirring the potatoes well every 10 minutes, until they are crisp and golden outside and tender inside, about 40 minutes.
- Sprinkle the potatoes with the salt and the parsley if you are using it, then season them with pepper to taste. Toss again and serve immediately.

Double-Hominy Grits with Cheese and Green Onions

Serves 8

Unreconstructed southerners will argue that grits is supposed to be bland, absorbing lots of butter and releasing endorphins of comfort while engaging the taste buds not at all. Contrary Yankee that I am, I think a little boost of flavor is called for, which explains this lively morning side dish. Try it with eggs and panfried country ham steaks or Oven-Glazed Pepper Bacon (page 44), and be sure to set the hot-sauce bottle on the table.

3½ cups water

⅔ cup old-fashioned (not quick-cooking or instant) white hominy grits

¾ teaspoon salt

1 can (16 ounces) white or yellow hominy, drained

½ cup thinly sliced green onions

½ teaspoon freshly ground black pepper

¼ pound sharp Cheddar or jalapeño jack cheese, coarsely shredded (about 1 cup)

- In a heavy saucepan over high heat, bring the water to a boil. Stir in the grits and salt and return to a boil. Lower the heat, cover partially, and simmer, stirring occasionally, for 12 minutes.
- Meanwhile, in a food processor, using short bursts of power, chop the hominy to coarse bits the size of peas.
- Stir the chopped hominy, ⅓ cup of the onions, and the pepper into the grits. Cover partially and continue to cook, stirring often, until very thick, about 8 minutes.
- Remove the pan from the heat, stir in the cheese, and let stand, covered, for 1 minute. Stir to blend. Sprinkle the remaining onions over the grits and serve immediately.

Borrowed Home Fries

Serves 4 to 6

This crusty side dish, which includes plenty of browned peppers, mushrooms, and onions in among the potatoes, was inspired by one served at the regional Keüken Dutch restaurant chain. There, the home fries frequently come napped with hollandaise sauce, an enrichment that shocks even me. Don't rule it out, but do try them plain, first: They're excellent. Success in making home fries, by the way, lies in not stirring them too often, which lets them brown nicely.

The Night Before

- In a large pot, cover the potatoes with cold water. Add I tablespoon salt, set over medium heat, and bring to a boil. Cook until almost done through while still showing slight resistance when pierced with a knife, about 30 minutes. Drain, let cool, wrap well, and refrigerate.
- In a large, heavy skillet over medium heat, warm 2 tablespoons of the bacon drippings. Add the onions and red pepper, cover, and cook, stirring occasionally, for 5 minutes. Add the mushrooms and ½ teaspoon salt and cook, covered, until the mushrooms begin to render their juices, about 5 minutes. Uncover the skillet, raise the heat to high, and cook, stirring often, until the mushroom juices have evaporated and the vegetables are lightly browned, 4 to 6 minutes. Remove from the heat and let cool completely. Cover and refrigerate.

In the Morning

- Peel the potatoes and cut them into ½-inch chunks.
- In a large, heavy skillet over medium heat, warm the remaining 3 tablespoons bacon drippings. Add the potatoes and cook, lifting and turning them with a spatula every 5 to 7 minutes, until they are crisp and golden, about 20 minutes. Add the mushroom mixture and ¾ teaspoon salt and continue to cook, stirring only occasionally, until the potatoes are browned and tender, another 5 to 7 minutes. Season generously with black pepper and serve hot.

2½ **pounds (5 medium) red-skinned potatoes**

Salt

5 **tablespoons bacon drippings, olive oil, or corn oil**

2 **cups chopped yellow onions**

I **large red sweet pepper, stemmed, cored, and finely diced**

½ **pound fresh brown (cremini) or white mushrooms, wiped clean and coarsely chopped**

Freshly ground black pepper

Quick, Rich Refried Beans

Serves 4

Making refried beans is a low-tech, but lengthy operation, one I sometimes skip in favor of these easy boosted beans, which are ready about the same time as the eggs are.

- In a heavy saucepan over low heat, combine the refried beans, black beans, and bacon drippings. Cover and cook, stirring often, until heated through and steaming, about 5 minutes. Serve hot.

I **can (16 ounces) refried black beans**

I **cup drained canned black beans, rinsed**

2 **tablespoons bacon drippings, unsalted butter, or olive oil**

Creamed Hash Browns

Serves 6 to 8

Few skillets full of potatoes are as enticing as these—partially crusty, partially creamy, lightly scented with onion. Figure on the recipe serving eight if you do the dishing up; if guests are left to their own portion control, count on it serving six, maybe even fewer.

2½ pounds (5 medium) red-skinned
   potatoes
Salt
4 tablespoons (½ stick) unsalted
   butter
½ cup finely chopped yellow onions
Freshly ground black pepper
1 cup whipping cream

The Night Before
■ In a large pot, cover the potatoes with cold water. Add 1 tablespoon salt, set over medium heat, and bring to a boil. Cook until the potatoes are almost done through while still showing slight resistance at their centers when pierced with a knife, about 30 minutes. Drain, let cool, wrap well, and refrigerate.

In the Morning
■ Peel the potatoes and coarsely shred them. In a large, heavy skillet over low heat, melt the butter. Add the onions, cover, and cook, stirring occasionally, until tender, about 10 minutes. Spread half the shredded potatoes in the skillet and sprinkle them evenly with ¼ teaspoon salt. Spread the remaining potatoes in the skillet and sprinkle them evenly with ¼ teaspoon salt. Cook uncovered, without stirring, until lightly browned on the bottom, about 6 minutes.
■ Turn and stir the potatoes thoroughly. Season them generously with pepper. Drizzle them with half the cream and cook without stirring until lightly browned on the bottom, about 4 minutes. Turn and stir the potatoes again, drizzle them with the remaining ½ cup cream, and cook for 2 minutes. Stir the potatoes and cook until most of the cream has been absorbed and the potatoes are crusty and tender, another 2 minutes. Serve immediately.

Dirty Rice

Serves 4 to 6

Rice and eggs may not be mainstream American, but in certain homes, in certain regions, early eaters wouldn't have it any other way. This Cajun rice dish, nubbly and brown with bits of chicken gizzards, hearts, and livers if you like, is among the liveliest of such treatments, and one that I, who doesn't need my breakfast bland, wholeheartedly endorse. Serve the rice with scrambled eggs, a big slice of panfried country ham, and strong chicory-boosted coffee.

- Pat the hearts and gizzards dry. In a heavy saucepan over medium heat, melt the bacon drippings. Add the giblets and cook, stirring once or twice, until well browned, about 10 minutes. With a slotted spoon, transfer the hearts and gizzards to a plate and let cool.
- Add the red pepper, onions, garlic, thyme, oregano, cumin, black pepper, cayenne pepper, and bay leaf to the saucepan. Cover, lower the heat, and cook, stirring often and scraping up the browned bits on the bottom, until tender, about 10 minutes.
- Meanwhile, in a food processor, finely chop the hearts and gizzards. Add them to the saucepan along with the water and salt and bring to a simmer. Stir in the rice, cover, and cook for 20 minutes. If you are using the chicken livers, spread them over the top of the rice now. Cover the pan and cook another 5 minutes, or until all the water has been absorbed and steam holes have appeared in the rice.
- Remove from the heat and let stand for 5 minutes. Stir the chicken livers into the rice; discard the bay leaf. Serve hot.

½ **pound mixed chicken hearts and gizzards**
3 **tablespoons bacon drippings or olive oil**
¾ **cup chopped red sweet pepper**
½ **cup thinly sliced green onions**
3 **garlic cloves, finely chopped**
¾ **teaspoon dried thyme, crumbled**
½ **teaspoon dried oregano, crumbled**
½ **teaspoon ground cumin**
½ **teaspoon freshly ground black pepper**
¼ **teaspoon cayenne pepper**
1 **bay leaf**
2¼ **cups water**
¾ **teaspoon salt**
1 **cup converted rice**
About ⅓ **pound chicken livers, diced (optional)**

FRUITS AND JUICES

Strawberry-Rhubarb Sauce

Makes 4 cups

In my family's kitchen parlance, rhubarb sauce is actually stewed rhubarb, a tart compote enjoyed cold from a bowl with a spoon, before getting on to other, more serious breakfast items. In fact, it also makes a good sauce-as-sauce, spooned over waffles, pancakes, blintzes, even ice cream, if you love rhubarb as much as I do. Stirring in fresh strawberries near the end of cooking gives the sauce a rosy hue and a lovely, old-fashioned summertime flavor.

- In a nonreactive saucepan over low heat, combine the rhubarb, sugar, and water. Bring to a simmer, skimming any scum that forms. Cover partially and cook until the rhubarb is almost tender, 15 to 20 minutes. Add the strawberries and cook until the sauce is rosy and thick, about 5 minutes.
- Remove from the heat and let cool to room temperature. Stir in the lemon juice. Cover and refrigerate. Serve the sauce cold if it is to be eaten as is, or rewarm over low heat if it will be used as a topping.

4 cups cubed rhubarb (½-inch cubes; from about 1 pound fresh stalks), or an equal amount frozen unsweetened rhubarb, thawed, with juices

3 cups sugar

2 cups water

2 cups cut-up stemmed strawberries (½-inch chunks; from about 1 pound berries)

3 tablespoons fresh lemon juice

Blueberry-Watermelon Smoothie

Serves 1 or 2

This icy magenta fruit shake is wonderfully intense, since frozen blueberries serve as both a chilling agent and a main ingredient. (There is thus no ice to dilute the flavor.) The amounts of lemon juice and honey called for suit my taste, but feel free to adjust either, depending upon the sweetness of the fruit you use.

- In a blender, combine all the ingredients. Partially chop with short bursts of power, then purée on high until smooth. Adjust the seasoning to taste.
- Pour the smoothie into 1 or 2 glasses and serve immediately.

2 cups cut-up seedless watermelon (1-inch chunks)

1 cup frozen blueberries, unthawed

2 tablespoons fresh lemon juice

2 tablespoons honey

Strawberry-Pineapple Compote

Serves 4

This is fresh, quick, and colorful. The rum can be omitted, if desired, and other berries can be used in place of the strawberries.

1 pint strawberries, rinsed only if
   necessary, stemmed and
   quartered
½ medium pineapple, cored, peeled,
   and cut into ½-inch chunks (about
   2 cups)
¼ cup fresh orange juice
3 tablespoons Meyer's dark rum
1 tablespoon fresh lemon juice
1 cup plain yogurt, regular or nonfat
4 fresh mint sprigs, for garnish

■ In a bowl, combine the strawberries, pineapple, orange juice, rum, and lemon juice. Cover and let stand at room temperature, stirring once or twice, for 30 minutes.

■ Spoon the fruit into 4 stemmed goblets, dividing it evenly. Spoon any juices from the bowl evenly over the fruit. Top the fruit with the yogurt, dividing it evenly. Garnish each serving with a mint sprig and serve immediately.

Orange-Stewed Prunes

Serves 6

Half the pleasure of stewed prunes is the delicious syrup produced by the stewing, hence this honey-sweetened, vanilla-scented version. The other half of the pleasure is knowing the prunes keep, moist and cool in the refrigerator, for up to ten days, and can help transform even a piece of toast and an egg into something special.

1 pound unpitted prunes
3 cups fresh orange juice
1½ cups water
½ cup honey
1 vanilla bean, halved crosswise,
   then split lengthwise

■ In a saucepan, combine the prunes, orange juice, water, honey, and vanilla bean. Set over medium heat and bring to a boil, skimming the foam that forms on the surface of the liquid. Lower the heat slightly, and simmer uncovered, gently stirring several times, until the prunes are tender and the liquid is reduced by half, about 20 minutes.

■ Remove from the heat, let cool to room temperature, and refrigerate for at least 24 hours before serving. Serve cold.

Baked Bananas

Serves 4

Bananas are so darned good for you, eating them seems more like work than play. One way to add some pleasure to the nutritional pump-up is to bake them in a tart-sweet glaze of orange juice. Eaten before, after, or as breakfast, these bananas are too good to be good for you.

- Position a rack in the middle of the oven and preheat to 400 degrees F.
- Arrange the bananas in a single layer in a shallow baking dish just large enough to hold them. Pour the orange juice over the bananas. Sprinkle the brown sugar over the bananas. Scatter the butter over the bananas. Bake, basting occasionally, until the bananas are very tender and the sauce is partially reduced, about 25 minutes.
- Carefully transfer the bananas to plates. Return the baking dish to the oven and bake until the sauce is further reduced and thickened, about 5 minutes. Spoon the sauce over the bananas. Serve hot or warm.

4 large, firm bananas, peeled
½ cup fresh orange juice
2 tablespoons packed light brown sugar
2 tablespoons unsalted butter, cut into small pieces

SAUCES, SYRUPS, CONDIMENTS, AND PRESERVES

Cafe Pasqual's Red Chile Sauce

Makes about 4 cups

The finest chiles in the land come from New Mexico, and I urge you to track them down. A blend of hot and mild pods is desirable, not only for keeping a sensible lid on the heat level of morning food, but for increased complexity of taste as well. Pasqual's red chile makes a fine sauce for enchiladas and burritos, or can be used as a braising medium for chicken or pork.

6 ounces dried mild New Mexico red chiles

6 ounces dried hot New Mexico red chiles

1 medium-large yellow onion (about ¾ pound), finely chopped

8 garlic cloves

1 tablespoon dried oregano, preferably Mexican, crumbled

2 teaspoons ground cumin

Salt

About 1 tablespoon packed dark brown sugar

■ Using kitchen scissors, stem the chiles, split them open, and scrape out the seeds. Cut the chile flesh into 1-inch pieces.

■ In a large, heavy saucepan, add enough hot tap water to the chile pieces just to cover them. Put the lid on the pot and let stand, stirring occasionally, until cool.

■ Add the onion, garlic, oregano, cumin, and 2 teaspoons salt, and set the pot over medium heat. Simmer uncovered, stirring occasionally, until very tender, about 20 minutes.

■ Cool slightly, then drain, reserving the liquid. Working in batches, in a food processor purée the chile pieces, adding enough reserved liquid to each batch to allow efficient processing (about ½ cup). Set a sieve over a bowl. With a flexible spatula, force the purée through the sieve into the bowl; discard the tough bits of skin and the seeds that remain in the sieve.

■ In a saucepan, stir enough of the remaining reserved chile liquid (you may use as much as 2 cups) into the purée to form a sauce about the thickness of ketchup. Taste and adjust the seasoning, adding salt and brown sugar to balance the chiles' natural bitterness.

■ Let cool completely, cover, and refrigerate for up to 3 days, or freeze for up to 2 months. Rewarm the sauce over low heat, stirring often to prevent scorching, before using.

Fresh Blackberry Sauce

Makes about 2 cups

Barely cooked, this sauce retains all the tartness of the fresh berries, just smoothed slightly and tamed. It's wonderful with the creole rice fritters on page 14, but equally good over pancakes, waffles, or the crêpe stack on page 98.

3 containers (6 ounces each) blackberries, picked over

About ¼ cup sugar

1 tablespoon fresh orange juice

1 tablespoon cornstarch

■ In a food processor, combine the berries and ½ cup of the sugar. Process until smooth. Force the purée through a sieve into a medium, nonreactive saucepan. Bring just to a simmer, stirring often.

■ Meanwhile, in a small bowl, stir the orange juice into the cornstarch. Stir the cornstarch mixture into the sauce and simmer until thick and clear, about 30 seconds. Remove from the heat and adjust the seasoning, adding additional sugar to taste. Cool and refrigerate the sauce for up to 3 days; rewarm it over low heat before serving.

Amy's Pepper Jelly Syrup

Makes about 2 cups

The last time I used this delicious sweet-and-fiery syrup in a cookbook I forgot the orange juice. Here to correct the matter is the official version, passed on to me years ago by Amy Lamphere, a fine midwestern cook. For the best flavor and appearance, choose a very spicy jelly that is not artificially colored (or is at least artificially red, not green, which makes for bilious-looking syrup). Serve it over cornmeal-based pancakes or waffles, or use it to enliven traditional French toast.

- In a small, heavy saucepan over low heat, combine the jelly, orange juice, butter, and honey. Heat, stirring often, until smooth. Use hot.
- ■ Note: Leftover syrup can be cooled, covered, and refrigerated for up to 1 week. Rewarm over low heat until smooth before using.

1 jar (10 ounces) hot pepper jelly (about 1 cup)
⅓ cup fresh orange juice
4 tablespoons (½ stick) unsalted butter
2 tablespoons honey

Marmalade Butter

Makes about ⅔ cup

Choose a sweeter American marmalade or a more bitter English one, according to your taste.

- In a small bowl, stir together the butter, marmalade, and sugar. Cover and refrigerate until serving.
- Bring to room temperature before using.

6 tablespoons (¾ stick) unsalted butter, at room temperature
⅓ cup orange marmalade
1 tablespoon confectioners' sugar

Toasted Hazelnut Butter

Makes about 1 cup

A few tablespoons of Frangelico or another hazelnut liqueur will boost the butter's flavor, but its use is entirely optional.

½ cup unblanched hazelnuts

8 tablespoons (1 stick) unsalted
   butter, softened

2 tablespoons packed light brown
   sugar

2 tablespoons Frangelico or other
   hazelnut liqueur (optional)

The Night Before

■ Position a rack in the middle of the oven and preheat to 375 degrees F. Spread the hazelnuts in a single layer in a shallow metal pan and toast them, stirring once or twice, until lightly browned and fragrant, 8 to 10 minutes. Wrap the hot hazelnuts in a clean towel and let steam for 1 minute. Rub the towel-wrapped hazelnuts vigorously between your palms to remove as much of their skins as possible. Shake the nuts in a colander to separate them from the skins. Let cool completely. Store airtight at room temperature.

In the Morning

■ Coarsely chop the hazelnuts. In a bowl, stir together the hazelnuts, butter, brown sugar, and the liqueur, if using. Use the butter within an hour or so, or the hazelnuts will become soft.

Plum and Apple Butter

Makes about 3 pints

The time for making this tart ruby preserve is mid- to late summer, when red plums and apples are in the market simultaneously. A food mill (preferably of stainless steel with interchangeable blades) is required if the butter is to have the right luscious, velvety texture.

2 pounds slightly underripe,
   unpeeled red plums such as Santa
   Rosa, quartered and pitted

2 pounds unpeeled, uncored
   Jonathan or McIntosh apples,
   stemmed and quartered

2 cups fresh unfiltered,
   unsweetened apple juice

2 cups sugar

2 teaspoons ground cinnamon

2 teaspoons vanilla extract

■ In a heavy, nonreactive pan, combine the plums, apples, and apple juice. Set over medium heat and bring to a boil. Lower the heat, cover partially, and simmer, stirring occasionally, for 25 minutes. Uncover and cook, stirring occasionally, until the apples are very tender, 20 to 30 minutes. Let cool slightly.

■ Force the fruit mixture through a food mill fitted with the medium blade. Discard the skins and seeds. Return the purée to the pan. Add the sugar and cinnamon and stir very well (undissolved sugar will burn onto the bottom of the pan). Set over medium heat and bring to a boil, stirring constantly. Lower the heat slightly and simmer briskly, stirring often, until the butter is thick and glossy, about 40 minutes.

■ Remove from the heat and stir in the vanilla. Spoon the hot butter into hot, sterilized jars. Cool, cover, and refrigerate. Let the butter mellow for 1 week before using. The butter will keep for several months.

Orange Curd

Makes about 3 cups

Despite the cheesy name, curds are actually thick, rich custards, perfect spread onto pancakes, scones, or biscuits, or used as a dip for big beautiful strawberries. Various citrus curds—orange, lemon, lime—are available in jars from the gourmet shop (read the label, since many are full of fake things), but making one's own is easy and considerably less expensive.

- In a heavy, nonreactive saucepan, whisk together the eggs, egg yolks, sugar, orange juice, orange zest, and lemon juice. Set over low heat and cook, stirring constantly, until the mixture thickens and leaves a heavy track on the back of the spoon when a fingertip is drawn across it. This happens rather suddenly, after about 8 minutes.
- Immediately remove the pan from the heat, add the butter all at once, and stir until smooth. Stir in the liqueur, and let cool to room temperature. Cover with plastic wrap, pressing it onto the surface of the curd, and refrigerate. The curd will keep for up to 1 week.

4 **eggs**

4 **egg yolks**

½ **cup sugar**

½ **cup fresh orange juice**

¼ **cup minced orange zest (colored peel)**

3 **tablespoons fresh lemon juice**

8 **tablespoons (1 stick) chilled unsalted butter, cut into small pieces**

3 **tablespoons orange liqueur**

Helen Corbitt's Blueberry Sauce

Makes about 4 cups

Developed by Corbitt for use with the crêpe stack on page 98, this quick and convenient sauce, which uses frozen berries, has lots of morning-time uses, from pancakes, French toast and waffles to omelets. It can also dress up an ice cream sundae or pound cake. I have fortified the berry flavor slightly by adding a touch of crème de cassis (black currant liqueur). The sauce can be made a day or two in advance, but should be reheated just to a simmer right before use.

- In a small bowl, stir together the sugar and cornstarch. In a nonreactive saucepan, combine the reserved blueberry juices and the water. Set over medium heat. Gradually whisk the sugar mixture into the liquid. Bring to a simmer, lower the heat slightly, and cook until the sauce thickens and turns clear, about 1 minute. Stir in the berries and remove the sauce from the heat. Stir in the lemon juice and cassis. Serve hot.

⅓ **cup sugar**

3 **tablespoons cornstarch**

3 **bags (10 ounces each) frozen unsweetened blueberries, thawed, juices reserved**

1 **cup water**

2 **tablespoons fresh lemon juice**

2 **tablespoons crème de cassis**

Ginger-Pear Compote

Makes about 2 cups

Good warm spooned over pancakes, waffles, or French toast, or dolloped onto almost any hot cereal you can conceive (but especially the cornmeal mush on page 14), this gingery pear sauce is also nice cold, served as you would applesauce, as an accompaniment to a smoked ham or turkey or roast pork. And it makes a fine, not-too-sweet ice cream topping as well.

2 pounds (5 medium) firm but ripe Bartlett pears, cored, peeled, and cut into ½-inch chunks
⅓ cup sugar
¼ cup water
3 tablespoons fresh lemon juice
2 tablespoons grated ginger

■ In a nonreactive saucepan over medium heat, combine the pears, sugar, water, lemon juice, and ginger. Cover and bring to a simmer. Uncover and cook, stirring occasionally, until the pear chunks are tender but still discernible and the sauce has thickened slightly, about 25 minutes. Remove from the heat and let cool to room temperature. Refrigerate for 24 hours or up to 3 days before using. Serve hot or cold.

Mellow Morning Salsa

Makes about 2½ cups

Use only the reddest, ripest, most tomato-flavored tomatoes for this mellow salsa, one that has only minimal amounts of garlic, jalapeño, and cilantro. Boost those accordingly, if mellow is not your desire, and use the salsa on eggs, omelets, and so on (in my experience salsa lovers don't usually require a lot of serving tips).

1 yellow or red sweet pepper
3 tomatoes (about 1½ pounds), cored, juices and seeds squeezed out, and cut into 1-inch chunks
½ cup finely chopped yellow onions
1 fresh jalapeño chile, stemmed and chopped
1 garlic clove, minced
1 tablespoon fresh lime juice
¾ teaspoon salt
2 tablespoons finely chopped fresh cilantro

The Night Before
■ In the open flame of a gas burner or under a preheated broiler, roast the pepper, turning it occasionally, until the skin is lightly but evenly charred. Steam the pepper in a closed paper bag until cool. Rub away the burned skin, stem and seed the pepper, and finely dice.
■ In a food processor, combine the tomatoes, half the onions, the jalapeño, garlic, lime juice, and salt and process until fairly smooth. Transfer to a bowl. Stir in the diced sweet pepper and the remaining onion. Cover and refrigerate overnight.

In the Morning
■ Stir the cilantro into the salsa. Taste and adjust the seasoning before using.

Spicy Peach Ketchup

Makes about 3½ cups

Tomato ketchup now rules by default, but is descended from a longer line of tangy condiments that came originally from Indonesia and then were embraced by Edwardian and Victorian England. Dusky gold, moderately sweet and tart, and spiced with a light touch, this sauce is wonderful alongside ham or corned beef (any smoky or salty meat really), as well as rich fish like salmon.

4 cups sliced, peeled fresh peaches, or 2 bags (16 ounces each) thawed, frozen peaches, with their juices

¾ cup finely chopped yellow onions

⅔ cup sugar

⅔ cup cider vinegar

¾ teaspoon salt

½ teaspoon cayenne pepper

¼ teaspoon ground ginger

¼ teaspoon ground cinnamon

¼ teaspoon ground turmeric

¼ teaspoon ground cloves

■ In a heavy, nonreactive saucepan over medium heat, combine the peaches, onions, sugar, vinegar, salt, cayenne pepper, ginger, cinnamon, turmeric, and cloves. Bring to a simmer. Cover partially and cook, stirring occasionally, until the peaches are very tender and the ketchup has thickened, about 20 minutes.

■ Let cool slightly, then force through a food mill fitted with the medium blade, or purée in a food processor. Cover and refrigerate for at least 24 hours before using. The ketchup will keep for several weeks in the refrigerator or can be frozen for up to 3 months.

Cherry-Amaretto Sauce

Makes about 1¼ cups

This easy crimson pancake and waffle topping can be made with sour red or sweet black cherry preserves. Either way, select a brand that has the maximum amount of whole fruit. The amaretto is optional, but cherries, like most stone fruits, combine wonderfully with the flavor of almonds in any form.

■ In a small, heavy saucepan over low heat, combine the preserves, butter, lemon juice, and amaretto. Bring just to a simmer, stirring occasionally. Use the syrup hot. Unused syrup will keep for many weeks. Cover tightly and refrigerate; rewarm before using.

1 jar (12 ounces) good-quality sour red or sweet black cherry preserves
2 tablespoons unsalted butter
2 tablespoons fresh lemon juice
1 tablespoon amaretto (Italian almond liqueur), preferably Disaranno amaretto

BREAKFAST IS TUESDAY; BRUNCH IS SUNDAY. BREAKFAST IS PANCAKES; BRUNCH IS CREPES. BREAKFAST IS ORANGE JUICE; BRUNCH IS A SCREWDRIVER. BREAKFAST IS DOONESBURY, CATHY, AND DILBERT; BRUNCH IS VIVALDI, SINATRA, AND MARIAN MCPARTLAND. BREAKFAST CAN BE SOLITARY, BRUNCH REQUIRES A CROWD. BRUNCH IS BREAKFAST, WITH A SHAVE. ACTUALLY THERE IS SOME MOSTLY ONE-WAY CROSSOVER. BREAKFAST ITEMS MAY APPEAR AT BRUNCH, BUT BRUNCH DISHES ALMOST NEVER SHOW UP AT BREAKFAST. BREAKFAST IS A MEAL, BUT BRUNCH IS MORE A STATE OF MIND (I'VE SERVED IT AT FOUR IN THE AFTERNOON), AND AS LONG AS IT FEELS CELEBRATORY, EVEN IF THE MENU IS BACON, EGGS, HASH BROWNS, AND COFFEE, WITHOUT A DROP OF CHAMPAGNE IN SIGHT, IT'S BRUNCH. THAT SAID, SOME THINGS STILL DON'T BELONG (THIS LIST IS PROBABLY PERSONAL), WHICH IS WHY CHILI, PIZZA, AND LEG OF LAMB ARE MISSING FROM THE FOLLOWING SIX CHAPTERS, WHILE LITTLE GRILLED STEAKS, GRUYÈRE FONDUE, AND BROWNIES ARE INCLUDED. WHAT THERE IS IS PLENTY OF COMFORTABLE *LUXE*—SMOKED SALMON, CAVIAR, A GLAZED HAM, MAPLE-GLAZED CINNAMON ROLLS, WARM GINGERBREAD—PLUS JUST ENOUGH POTENT POTABLES TO MELLOW THE MOOD. IF IT'S BRUNCH, AFTER ALL, THE COUNTDOWN TO MONDAY IS ALREADY UNDERWAY, AND IT'S ONLY A MATTER OF TIME BEFORE REALITY RETURNS. WHICH CALLS, I THINK, FOR JUST A BIT MORE CHAMPAGNE.

BRUNCH

STARTERS

I

Crisp Potato Nests with Mascarpone and Caviar—page 84

Crab and Sweet Red Pepper Bisque

Serves 8

This elegant soup (which can be almost completely prepared in advance) is rich, but the portions are small. For a buffet meal, pass it in small coffee cups or, if the brunch is seated, serve it at the table in consommé bowls. Eastern blue crab meat or western Dungeness work equally well here. I've also enjoyed the soup with diced cooked lobster in place of crab.

3 tablespoons unsalted butter
1 cup chopped yellow onions
1 cup chopped celery
1 cup chopped red sweet pepper
1¼ teaspoons Old Bay Seasoning or other seafood spice mixture
3 cups fish stock or bottled clam juice
½ cup finely diced russet (baking) potato
¾ teaspoon salt
½ cup half-and-half
1 pound jumbo lump crab meat, picked over

The Night Before

■ In a saucepan over low heat, melt the butter. Add the onions, celery, red pepper and Old Bay; cover, and cook, stirring once or twice, for 10 minutes. Add the stock, potato, and salt and bring to a boil. Lower the heat, cover partially, and simmer, stirring once or twice, until the vegetables are very tender, about 25 minutes.

■ Remove from the heat and let cool slightly, then force the soup through a food mill fitted with the medium blade, or purée in a blender or food processor. Let cool to room temperature, cover and refrigerate.

In the Morning

■ In a saucepan combine the puréed soup and the half-and-half. Set over medium heat and bring to a simmer, stirring occasionally. Stir in the crab meat and heat for 30 seconds. Adjust the seasoning.

■ Remove from the heat, cover, and let stand for 1 minute. Serve hot.

Asparagus and Crab Meat Salads

Serves 4

Thick pink mayonnaise, full of sweet crab meat, is a great partner to cool green asparagus. Much like classic caviar-topped baked potatoes, this is a wonderful pairing of the rare and expensive with the (at least in spring) abundant and affordable—a state of affairs that usually leads to an increased appreciation of both elements. Diced cooked lobster meat can be substituted for the crab. Serve the salads for an elegant spring brunch, centered around a big glazed ham.

The Night Before
- In a small bowl, stir together the mayonnaise, lemon juice, tomato paste, shallots, mustard, and pepper. Cover tightly and refrigerate.

In the Morning
- Bring the mayonnaise just to room temperature.
- Bring a large pot three-fourths full of water to a boil. Add the salt and asparagus to the boiling water and cook uncovered, stirring once or twice, until just tender, about 4 minutes. Drain and immediately transfer to a large bowl of ice water. Let stand, stirring once or twice, until cold. Drain and pat dry.
- Stir the crab meat into the mayonnaise; adjust the seasoning. Divide the asparagus among 4 small plates. Spoon the crab mixture across the middle of the asparagus, dividing it evenly and using it all. Serve immediately.

1 cup mayonnaise
1 tablespoon fresh lemon juice
1½ teaspoons tomato paste
1½ teaspoons minced shallots
½ teaspoon Dijon mustard
¼ teaspoon freshly ground black pepper
1 tablespoon salt
1 pound asparagus, trimmed and peeled
Ice water
½ pound jumbo lump crab meat, picked over

Prosciutto with Pear, Fennel, and Walnut Salad

Serves 4

This is an easy starter for an autumn brunch, since most of the work is done by the Italian artisans who produce prosciutto according to a centuries-old method. The best comes from the area around Parma, in Emilia-Romagna (it will be so labeled), and while not inexpensive, a little of the translucent, meaty stuff goes a long way; please use it here if at all possible. (Volpi, from St. Louis, is a more-than-acceptable domestic substitute.) Follow the prosciutto with a meatless main dish, such as the mushroom pudding on page 99.

- In a bowl, combine the pear chunks and vinegar. Stir in the fennel, walnuts, olive oil, and fennel fronds. Season generously with freshly ground black pepper.
- On each of 4 plates, cross 2 slices of prosciutto to create an X. Spoon the pear mixture onto the centers of the Xs, dividing it evenly and using it all. Serve immediately.

1 large, ripe, juicy pear such as Bartlett, cored, peeled, and cut into ½-inch chunks
2 tablespoons Spanish sherry vinegar
½ cup coarsely chopped fennel bulb
⅓ cup coarsely chopped walnuts
¼ cup olive oil
1 tablespoon minced fennel fronds
Freshly ground black pepper
8 slices (about ½ pound) prosciutto, cut slightly thicker than usual, at room temperature

Crisp Potato Nests with Mascarpone and Caviar

Makes 24; serves 6 to 8

These crunchy little hash-brown cups, filled with rich Italian cream cheese and good caviar, manage to be both elegant and earthy. Serve them any time you feel like splurging a little, but especially for a Christmas or New Year's brunch. Use the tiniest possible muffin-tin cups to form the nests; the cups of the ones I have hold one tablespoon. For a festive effect, top the nests alternately with black sturgeon and red salmon caviars.

2 **medium-large russet (baking) potatoes**

4 **tablespoons (½ stick) unsalted butter, melted**

Freshly ground black pepper

About 3 ounces mascarpone cheese, at room temperature

2 **ounces good-quality black or red caviar**

The Night Before

■ In a saucepan, cover the potatoes with cold water. Set over medium heat and bring to a boil. Cook until the potatoes are half-done; a knife inserted into one should meet with considerable resistance. Drain, let cool, wrap well, and refrigerate.

In the Morning

■ Position a rack in the middle of the oven and preheat to 450 degrees F.

■ Peel the potatoes. On the large holes of a box grater, coarsely shred the potatoes. In a bowl, gently toss the shredded potatoes to mix the cooked and uncooked portions evenly.

■ With a pastry brush, butter the cups of 2 mini muffin tins (12 cups per tin). Divide the shredded potatoes among the cups (depending upon the tins you have you may not use all the potatoes), patting them lightly with a fingertip to form a small nest. (Some shreds extending over the edge of the edges of the cups are fine and make an interesting lacy effect on the finished nests.) Bake until the nests are crisp and golden and have pulled away slightly from the sides of the cups, 25 to 30 minutes.

■ Remove from the oven and let the potato nests rest in the tins on a rack for 5 minutes. Season generously with pepper. Using a blunt-tipped knife, remove the nests from the tins and transfer to a serving platter. Spoon a dollop of mascarpone into each nest (depending upon the tin you may not need all the mascarpone). Spoon a dollop of caviar atop each dollop of mascarpone. Serve immediately.

Gruyère Fondue
Serves 4

I love fondue, and so has every guest I've ever served it to, usually with the same sheepish pleasure that crosses adult faces on Christmas morning. Since this classic formula comes from the Wisconsin Milk Marketing Board, do make it at least once with domestic Gruyère; after that, experiment. One of the best fondues I ever ate was a mixture of two French cheeses—Comté and the luscious triple-crème, St.-André.

- Fill a bowl with cold water. Add the apple slices, pear slices, and 3 tablespoons plus 1 teaspoon of the lemon juice.
- Rub the inside surface of a fondue pot with the cut garlic halves. Light the heating element and adjust the flame to medium. Combine the wine and the remaining 2 teaspoons lemon juice in the fondue pot and bring to a simmer. In a bowl, toss together the Gruyère and cornstarch until well mixed. Gradually add the Gruyère mixture to the fondue pot, stirring constantly. Stir in the kirsch and heat without boiling until very thick, about 5 minutes.
- Meanwhile, drain the apple and pear slices and arrange on a plate with the grapes. Arrange the bread cubes in another container. Stir the nutmeg into the fondue and serve immediately. Provide long forks for dipping the fruits and bread cubes.

2 tart green apples, preferably Granny Smith, cored and sliced lengthwise

2 firm but ripe pears such as Bartlett, cored and sliced lengthwise

¼ cup fresh lemon juice

1 garlic clove, halved

1 cup medium-dry white wine such as Gewürztraminer

2 cups shredded Gruyère cheese

2 teaspoons cornstarch

1 tablespoon kirsch (unsweetened cherry brandy)

Seedless red and green grapes

Pinch of freshly grated nutmeg

1 loaf Cinnamon, Date, and Walnut Toasting Bread (page 50), or crusty walnut or plain bread, cut into 1-inch cubes, for dipping

Johnnycakes with Scallop and Smoked Salmon Ragout

Serves 8

The term johnnycake is generally considered to be a corruption of journey cake, a sort of sturdy, good-keeping, unleavened waybread for long-distance travelers in early America. These tender, red pepper–studded cornmeal pancakes, topped with a luscious seafood ragout, aren't intended to travel any farther than from plate to mouth, but will otherwise start a more formal brunch off with delicious style. Though the combination may at first sound odd to you, these are also good without the seafood ragout, slathered with plenty of sweet butter and maple syrup.

4 tablespoons (½ stick) unsalted butter

⅔ cup finely diced sweet red peppers

⅔ cup thinly sliced green onions

I cup fish stock or bottled clam juice

½ cup Chardonnay

Salt

Freshly ground white pepper

I pound bay scallops

3 tablespoons minced shallots

½ cup plus I tablespoon unbleached all-purpose flour

½ cup coarse yellow cornmeal, preferably stoneground

I teaspoon baking powder

2 eggs, separated, at room temperature

¾ cup milk

Canola or other flavorless oil or nonstick spray, for the griddle

¼ pound smoked salmon, in 8 very thin slices

Minced fresh chives, for garnish (optional)

- In a small skillet over medium heat, melt 3 tablespoons of the butter (let the remaining tablespoon of butter come to room temperature). Add the red peppers and cook uncovered, stirring once or twice, for 3 minutes. Add the green onions and cook uncovered, stirring once or twice, for 2 minutes. Remove from the heat and let cool to room temperature.

- In a nonreactive saucepan over medium heat, combine the stock, Chardonnay, a pinch of salt, and a generous grinding of pepper. Bring to a simmer. Add the scallops, lower the heat slightly, and cook, stirring once or twice, until the scallops are just opaque, 3 to 4 minutes. With a slotted spoon, transfer the scallops to a sieve set over a bowl. Add the shallots to the stock mixture and bring to a simmer. Cook uncovered until reduced to ¾ cup, about 15 minutes. Strain through a sieve into a small, nonreactive saucepan; discard the shallots. Set the stock mixture aside.

- Position a rack in the middle of the oven and preheat to 250 degrees F.

- Into a medium bowl, sift together twice the ½ cup flour, the cornmeal, baking powder, and ¼ teaspoon salt. In another medium bowl, whisk the egg whites to soft peaks. In a small bowl, whisk together the egg yolks and milk. Stir the milk mixture and half of the red pepper mixture into the dry ingredients. Fold the egg whites into the batter; do not overmix.

■ Set a large, preferably nonstick griddle or skillet over medium heat or preheat an electric griddle to 375 degrees F. When it is hot (test by flicking a few drops of water onto the griddle; they should skitter around briefly before evaporating), dip a folded paper towel into the oil and lightly brush the griddle. Spoon the batter onto the griddle, allowing 1½ tablespoons for each pancake. Cook for 1 to 1½ minutes. The pancakes will form a few bubbles on top. Use a spatula to check the undersides of the pancakes; they should be golden. Flip the pancakes and cook until they are just done through, about 1 minute longer. Keep the pancakes warm in the oven. Repeat with the remaining batter. There should be 24 small pancakes.

■ Meanwhile, in a small bowl, using a fork, mash together the remaining 1 tablespoon butter and 1 tablespoon flour to form a paste. Add any juices from the bowl below the scallops to the stock mixture and bring to a simmer over low heat. Whisk in the butter-flour paste, blending it in fully. Stir in the scallops and the remaining red pepper mixture and simmer, stirring often, until the sauce has thickened and the scallops are just heated through, about 1 minute.

■ Divide the pancakes among 8 small plates, placing 3 pancakes on each plate. Spoon the scallop mixture over the pancakes, dividing it evenly and using it all. Casually ruffle a slice of salmon atop each portion. Sprinkle with chives, if desired, and serve immediately.

SIDE AND MAIN DISH SALADS

2

Wilted Spinach Salad with Country Ham and Raisins

Serves 6

Crisp, nutty bits of Smithfield (or another good firm, smoky ham) and sweet, succulent raisins help renovate this old favorite into a compelling new salad.

5 tablespoons corn oil

1 cup (about ¼ pound) diced country ham (¼-inch dice)

3 pounds curly spinach, stemmed, well washed, and larger leaves torn into bite-sized pieces

1 small red onion, sliced and separated into rings

⅔ cup golden raisins

½ cup red wine vinegar

1 tablespoon sugar

Freshly ground black pepper

- In a nonreactive skillet over medium heat, combine the oil and ham. Cook uncovered, stirring occasionally, until the ham is lightly browned, 8 to 10 minutes.
- Meanwhile, place the spinach in a large bowl.
- Add the onion rings and raisins to the ham and cook, stirring, until the rings are almost tender, 4 to 5 minutes. Add the vinegar and sugar and bring just to a boil, stirring to dissolve the sugar and any browned bits from the bottom of the skillet.
- Pour the hot ham mixture over the spinach. Season generously with pepper and toss well. Divide the salad among serving plates. Spoon any dressing remaining in the bowl over the salads and serve immediately.

Watercress, Pink Grapefruit, and Avocado Salad

Serves 4

Brightly colorful, tartly refreshing, and with a touch of luscious avocado, this is my favorite, all-purpose brunch salad, perfect for starting almost any menu. In this recipe I call for tossing everything together and plating the salads individually, but sometimes I mound the cress on a platter and arrange the avocado wedges and grapefruit sections over it.

1 large pink grapefruit

2 bunches watercress, tough stems removed (about 7 cups)

3 tablespoons delicate olive oil or corn oil

Salt

1½ tablespoons Champagne or white tarragon vinegar

Freshly ground black pepper

1 black-skinned (Haas) avocado, pitted, peeled, and cut into wedges

- With a serrated knife, cut a thick slice off the top and bottom of the grapefruit, exposing the flesh. With the knife, cut down the sides of the grapefruit, following the natural curve, removing all the peel and bitter white pith. Holding the fruit over a bowl, cut along the membrane on either side of each section, allowing the fruit to fall into the bowl.
- In a large bowl, toss the watercress with the oil. Season with a sprinkle of salt and toss again. Add the vinegar, season with pepper, and toss again. Add the grapefruit sections and avocado wedges and toss gently. Spoon onto plates, dividing evenly, and serve immediately.

Shrimp Caesar Salad

Serves 4 to 6

Tinkering with a classic dish is usually risky, but in the case of the embellished Caesar salad, something good and new has been made out of something good and familiar. Among the possible enhancements—crisp fried calamari, grilled chicken, lump crab meat—large poached shrimp are the least gimmicky, tasting as if they had been part of this zesty salad all along. The dressing, based on bottled mayonnaise, is not classic, but it alleviates salmonella worries and can be completed well in advance of serving.

The Night Before

- Separate the romaine into leaves, discarding any tough outer leaves or yellowed leaves. Tear the inner leaves into bite-sized pieces. Wash well and spin dry. Wrap and refrigerate.
- Mince 3 of the garlic cloves. In a blender or small food processor, combine the mayonnaise, anchovy fillets, the minced garlic, the 2 tablespoons Parmigiano, the lemon juice, Worcestershire sauce, and mustard. Process until smooth. Season generously with freshly ground pepper and process again to blend. Cover and refrigerate.

In the Morning

- Bring a large pot three-fourths full of water to a boil. Stir in the salt, add the shrimp, and cook, stirring once or twice, until the shrimp are curled, pink, and just cooked through, about 2 minutes (the water need not even return to the boil). Drain immediately and let cool to room temperature.
- In a large skillet over low heat, warm the olive oil. Lightly crush the remaining 3 garlic cloves and add them to the oil. Cook, stirring and turning occasionally, until they are medium brown, about 8 minutes. Remove them with a slotted spoon and discard. Add the bread cubes to the skillet all at once and toss thoroughly to coat evenly with the oil. Cook the croutons, continuing to toss them, until they are evenly golden brown, 8 to 10 minutes. Remove from the heat, season to taste with pepper, and reserve at room temperature.
- In a large bowl, combine the romaine, shrimp, and mayonnaise dressing and toss thoroughly. Add the ⅓ cup Parmigiano and the croutons and toss again. Season generously with pepper. Serve immediately.

2 heads romaine lettuce

6 garlic cloves

¾ cup mayonnaise

4 caper-stuffed oil-packed anchovy fillets, drained and minced

2 tablespoons plus ⅓ cup grated Parmigiano Reggiano cheese

1 tablespoon fresh lemon juice

1 teaspoon Worcestershire sauce

1 teaspoon Dijon mustard

Freshly ground black pepper

1 tablespoon salt

1½ pounds (about 24) large shrimp, shelled and deveined

3 tablespoons olive oil

1½ cups cubed day-old bread (¾-inch cubes)

Retro Curried Chicken Salad
Serves 6

Dating from a time when American cooking was relatively spice free, this deliciously goopy salad, with its "exotic" curry flavor, now strikes a familiarly comfy note—perfect brunch food. There may be more fashionable chicken salads around, but there are few that will disappear so quickly. Cooking the curry powder in oil before stirring it into the dressing smooths the flavor, but the step, and the oil, are optional.

3 **tablespoons curry powder**
2 **tablespoons corn oil**
I **cup mayonnaise**
½ **cup sour cream**
¼ **cup honey mustard**
2 **tablespoons fresh lemon juice**
2½ **pounds boneless, skinless chicken breasts**
Salt
2 **cups seedless red grapes**
½ **cup diced red onions**
⅓ **cup sweetened flaked coconut**
⅔ **cup coarsely chopped peanuts**
Red-leaf lettuce and watercress, for garnish (optional)
⅔ **cup roasted skinless peanuts**
Mango chutney, for serving (optional)

The Night Before
■ In a small saucepan over low heat, combine the curry powder and oil. Cook, stirring, for 2 minutes. Remove from the heat and let cool.
■ In a bowl, whisk together the mayonnaise, sour cream, honey mustard, cooled curry mixture, and lemon juice. Cover and refrigerate.

In the Morning
■ Arrange the chicken breasts in a large, deep skillet that will just hold them in a single layer. Add cold water to cover. Evenly sprinkle in 2 teaspoons salt and set over medium heat. Bring slowly to a simmer, turning the chicken breasts once. Continue to simmer until just cooked through, about 5 minutes (check the chicken breasts for doneness at their thickest point by piercing with a small knife). Remove the skillet from the heat and let the chicken cool to room temperature in the poaching liquid. With a slotted spoon, transfer the chicken breasts to a cutting board and pat dry. Trim any fat or cartilage and cut the meat into ¾-inch cubes.
■ In a large bowl, stir together the chicken, mayonnaise dressing, grapes, onions, and coconut. Line a platter with lettuce and watercress, if desired. Spoon the salad into the center of the platter. Sprinkle the peanuts over the salad and serve, accompanied with the chutney, if desired.

Pistachio Rice Salad
Serves 6 to 8

This simple salad is a natural partner to the curried chicken salad at left, and will also serve nicely alongside a ham or a platter of smoked turkey or fish.

- In a saucepan over high heat, bring the water to a boil. Stir in the rice and salt. Cover, reduce the heat to low, and cook the rice undisturbed until it has absorbed all the water and is tender, about 22 minutes. Remove the pan from the heat and let stand, covered, for 5 minutes.
- Transfer the hot rice to a bowl and fluff with a fork. Add the orange juice, currants, lemon juice, and orange zest and fluff again. Let the rice stand, stirring it once or twice, until cool. Add the pistachios and the oil, season generously with pepper, and toss.
- Transfer to a bowl or platter. Serve at room temperature.

2½ cups water
1¼ cups long-grain white rice
1½ teaspoons salt
⅓ cup fresh orange juice
⅓ cup dried currants
1 tablespoon fresh lemon juice
1 tablespoon minced orange zest (colored peel)
½ cup coarsely chopped pistachios (from about 5 ounces unshelled nuts)
⅓ cup corn oil
Freshly ground black pepper

Warm Salad of Scrambled Eggs, Smoked Fish, and Greens
Serves 4

Served in smaller portions, this makes a good first course for a more elaborate brunch, but I like it better as the main dish, accompanied by split, toasted bagels and beer or Champagne.

2 medium bunches spinach, about
  1 ½ pounds total

1 head Boston lettuce

3 tablespoons white wine vinegar

2 tablespoons Dijon mustard

1 tablespoon sugar

Salt

½ cup corn or other flavorless oil

¼ cup whipping cream

¼ cup minced fresh dill

8 eggs

Freshly ground black pepper

4 tablespoons (½ stick) unsalted
  butter

⅓ pound smoked salmon, whitefish,
  sturgeon, or trout, thinly sliced or
  flaked

1 small red onion, thinly sliced and
  separated into rings

The Night Before
■ Discard any yellowed spinach leaves, then stem the spinach. Separate the lettuce head into leaves, discarding any tough outer leaves. Tear the greens into bite-sized pieces. Wash well and spin dry. Wrap and refrigerate.

In the Morning
■ In a small, nonreactive saucepan, whisk together the vinegar, mustard, sugar, and a pinch of salt. Gradually whisk in the oil and then the cream. Set over low heat and bring to just below a simmer. Stir in the dill, remove the pan from the heat, and cover to keep warm.

■ Divide the greens among 6 plates. In a bowl, briefly whisk together the eggs, ½ teaspoon salt, and pepper to taste. In a skillet over medium heat, melt the butter. Add the eggs and cook, stirring often, until softly set, 3 to 4 minutes.

■ Immediately spoon the hot eggs atop the greens, dividing them evenly. Top the eggs with the smoked fish. Spoon the warm dressing over the eggs and greens. Scatter the onion rings over the salads and serve immediately.

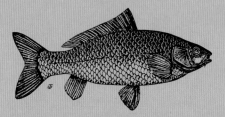

Sausage, Pepper, and Potato Frittata Smothered with Green Salad—page 103

Helen Corbitt's Lemon-Blueberry Crêpe Stack

Serves 8

This many-layered tower of large, thickish crêpes, filled with tangy lemon butter and blueberry sauce, then cut into wedges for serving, is one of Helen Corbitt's great creations, and is adapted from her book, *Helen Corbitt Cooks for Company*. Everyone loves it, says Corbitt, even "the young fry and the debutantes." As a caterer and restaurateur, especially at the famed Neiman-Marcus Zodiac Room, she influenced several generations of great home cooks, not just those from her home state of Texas. Grab any of her books you find at yard sales or in used bookstores; they're packed with great ideas. Serve the crêpe stack alongside ham, sausage, or bacon and eggs, on a dressy brunch buffet.

Lemon Butter

- 8 tablespoons (I stick) unsalted butter, at room temperature
- 2 tablespoons minced lemon zest (colored peel)
- 2½ cups confectioners' sugar
- 3 tablespoons fresh lemon juice

Crêpes

- 2⅓ cups unbleached all-purpose flour (see Note)
- ¼ cup sugar
- 4 teaspoons baking powder
- ½ teaspoon salt
- 2 eggs, at room temperature
- 2½ cups milk, at room temperature
- 4 tablespoons (½ stick) unsalted butter, melted
- Canola or other flavorless oil or nonstick spray, for the skillet
- Helen Corbitt's Blueberry Sauce (page 73), heated to simmer

The Night Before

■ For the lemon butter, in a bowl, with the back of a spoon, mash together thoroughly the butter and lemon zest. Stir in 1 cup of the confectioners' sugar. Stir in the lemon juice and mix. Add the remaining confectioners' sugar and mix until smooth. Cover and refrigerate.

In the Morning

■ Position a rack in the middle of the oven and preheat to 250 degrees F. Soften the lemon butter slightly at room temperature.

■ For the crêpes, into a large bowl, sift together twice the flour, sugar, baking powder, and salt. In a smaller bowl, whisk the eggs. Whisk in the milk and melted butter. Add the egg mixture to the flour mixture and whisk until smooth. The batter will be thin.

■ Heat a large, heavy, preferably nonstick skillet with a bottom diameter of 9 inches over low heat. Dip a paper towel into the oil and lightly coat the skillet. Add 1 cup batter to the skillet. Tilt and tip the skillet to coat the bottom evenly with batter. Bubbles will appear almost instantly on the crêpe. Continue to cook until it is almost fully done and lightly browned, about 3 minutes. Carefully turn the crêpe (a big spatula helps) and cook for another minute. Lay a sheet of waxed paper on a baking sheet. Transfer the crêpe to the waxed paper. Top with another piece of waxed paper and set the baking sheet in the oven. Repeat with the remaining batter, oiling the pan lightly between crêpes, layering the crêpes with waxed paper, and keeping them warm in the oven. There should be 8 crêpes in all (don't discard any torn or damaged ones; they will work fine in the stack).

■ Select a large, round, flat platter. Lay a crêpe on the platter. Spread it randomly with about 1½ tablespoons of the lemon butter. Drizzle it randomly with about ¼ cup of the blueberry sauce. Repeat with the remaining crêpes, drizzling ½ cup blueberry sauce over the topmost crêpe and centering the remaining butter in a dollop atop the sauce.

■ Cut the stack into wedges and serve, accompanied with remaining blueberry sauce.

■■ Note: To measure the flour, stir it in the canister with a fork to lighten, then spoon into dry-measure cups and sweep level.

Tarragon-Mushroom Bread Pudding

Serves 8 as a main course, 12 as a side dish

Descended from the long line of egg-and-bread custard casseroles known as *strata,* this madeira- and-tarragon-scented mushroom dish makes a fine brunch main course. It also doubles as an excellent side dish and tastes just great alongside a glazed ham (or at another meal altogether, accompanying a crisply roasted Sunday supper chicken). The pudding will be best when made with such assertive cultivated mushrooms as shiitakes and cremini.

The Night Before

■ In a large skillet over medium heat, melt the butter. Add the green onions and tarragon, cover, and cook, stirring occasionally, for 5 minutes. Add the shiitakes and cremini, sprinkle them with the salt, and cook, covered, stirring occasionally, until the mushrooms begin to render their juices and are becoming tender, about 7 minutes. Add the Madeira, raise the heat to high, and cook uncovered, tossing and stirring the mushrooms often, until all the liquid has evaporated and the mushrooms are lightly browned, 10 to 12 minutes. Remove from the heat and let cool to room temperature. Cover and refrigerate.

In the Morning

■ Butter a 9-by-13-inch baking dish. Position a rack in the middle of the oven and preheat to 350 degrees F (325 degrees F if the baking dish is of glass).

■ In a very large bowl, thoroughly whisk the eggs. Whisk in the cream and pepper sauce. With a serrated knife, trim off the ends of the bread loaves. Cut the bread on the diagonal into 1-inch-thick slices. Add the bread slices to the egg mixture and let stand, gently stirring occasionally, until the bread is moist and soft.

■ Arrange half the bread slices in a single layer over the bottom of the prepared baking dish. Spoon half the mushroom mixture evenly over the bread. Arrange the remaining bread in a single layer over the mushrooms. Spoon the remaining mushrooms over the final layer of bread. Pour any egg mixture remaining in the dish evenly over all.

■ Bake the pudding until it is puffed and golden and the center is just set without becoming grainy, 40 to 50 minutes. Remove from the oven and let the pudding stand in the dish on a rack for at least 10 minutes. Serve hot or warm.

5 tablespoons unsalted butter, plus softened butter for the baking dish

1 cup thinly sliced green onions

2 tablespoons dried tarragon, crumbled

1¼ pounds fresh shiitake mushrooms, wiped clean, stemmed, and caps thinly sliced

1 pound fresh cremini mushrooms, wiped clean and thinly sliced

2½ teaspoons salt

½ cup medium-dry Madeira wine

10 eggs

4 cups whipping cream

2 teaspoons hot-pepper sauce such as Tabasco

2 long, slender loaves crusty French bread, each 14 inches long

Cheese Blintzes with Fruit Sauce

Makes 13; serves 6

Blintzes are light but satisfying, and much of the work gets done a day ahead. This classic is from Selma Brown Morrow, a recipe tester at *Bon Appétit* magazine, in which it originally appeared. The cook gets the extra blintz.

Filling

1¼ pounds hoop cheese, or 2 pounds nonfat cottage cheese

½ cup plus 1 tablespoon sugar

1½ teaspoons salt

2 extra-large eggs

Crêpes

1½ cups water

3 extra-large eggs

1½ cups sifted unbleached all-purpose flour

1 tablespoon sugar

¾ teaspoon salt

Canola or other flavorless oil or nonstick spray, for the crêpe pan, plus canola oil for frying the blintzes

One or more fruit sauces (Helen Corbitt's Blueberry sauce, page 73; Strawberry-Rhubarb Sauce, page 65; Fresh Blackberry Sauce, page 70; Ginger-Pear Compote, page 74), heated to a simmer

Sour cream

The Night Before

■ For the filling, if using cottage cheese, place it in the center of a kitchen towel, gather the towel around the cheese, and squeeze to remove the excess moisture. Measure out 2½ cups packed cottage cheese; reserve the remainder for another use. Combine the hoop cheese or the 2½ cups packed dry cottage cheese and the sugar in a food processor and blend well. Add the eggs and salt and process until almost smooth, scraping down the sides of the work bowl occasionally. Transfer to a bowl, cover, and refrigerate.

■ For the crêpes, combine the water and eggs in a blender. Add the flour, sugar, and salt. Blend on low speed until very smooth, stopping occasionally to scrape down the sides of the blender jar. Transfer to a bowl, cover, and let stand at room temperature for 1 hour.

■ Select a heavy, preferably nonstick skillet or crêpe pan 7 inches in diameter (or use a larger skillet and make somewhat more free-form crêpes). Set it over high heat. Dip a paper towel into the oil and lightly coat the skillet. Stir the batter, then measure out 3 tablespoons and pour into the center of the hot skillet. Working quickly, lift and tilt the skillet to spread the batter into a 7-inch round. Lower the heat to medium-high and cook until the bottom of the crêpe is speckled brown, about 45 seconds. Lay a sheet of waxed paper on a baking sheet. Transfer the crêpe to the waxed paper. Top with another piece of waxed paper. Repeat with the remaining batter, oiling the pan lightly between crêpes and layering the crêpes with waxed paper. There will be more than 13 crêpes; discard any that are torn or otherwise imperfect.

■ Lay 1 crêpe, cooked side up, on a work surface. Place ¼ cup filling in a 3-inch-long log just below the center. Fold the bottom of the crêpe over the filling. Fold the sides in and roll the crêpe up, enclosing the filling completely in a rectangular package. Transfer blintz to a plastic wrap–lined sheet pan. Repeat with remaining filling to make 13 blintzes. Cover and refrigerate.

In the Morning

■ Pour canola oil into 2 large, preferably nonstick skillets to a depth of ⅛ inch. Warm over medium-low heat until hot. Add the blintzes, seam side down, to the hot oil. Cook until bottoms are brown and crisp, shaking the pans gently and moving the blintzes occasionally to prevent sticking, about 6 minutes. With a spatula, turn the blintzes and cook until bottoms are brown and crisp and the blintzes feel firm when lightly pressed, about 5 minutes. Drain on paper towels.

■ Set 2 blintzes on each of 6 plates. Spoon about ½ cup warm fruit sauce over one serving, napping the blintzes partially. Top with a dollop of sour cream. Serve immediately. Repeat with the remaining blintzes, sauce, and sour cream.

Pasqual's Pan-Fried Polenta with Chorizo and Corn
Serves 6

This is my variation on a popular rib-sticking breakfast item from the menu of Cafe Pasqual, a Santa Fe institution. I have simplified the recipe somewhat from chef Katherine Kagel's published version, but the resulting dish is every bit as deliciously eye-opening as that served at the cafe. Although Kagel does not include it, a poached egg, set atop the polenta before the sauce is spooned over, is a worthy addition.

The Night Before

■ In the open flame of a gas burner or under a preheated broiler, roast the chiles, turning them occasionally, until the skins are lightly but evenly charred. Steam the chiles in a closed paper bag until cool. Rub away the burned skin, stem and seed the chiles, and then chop them. There should be about 1 cup.

■ Brush a 9-by-13-inch baking pan with 1 tablespoon of the olive oil. In a deep, heavy pot, slowly whisk the water into the cornmeal. Stir in 2 teaspoons salt. Set the pot over medium heat and bring to a simmer, whisking often. Cover partially and cook, stirring occasionally, until the cornmeal is very thick and is pulling away from the sides of the pot, about 30 minutes.

■ Remove from the heat. Stir in the green chiles. Pour the hot cornmeal into the prepared pan. Gently shake the pan to even the cornmeal; smooth the top with the back of a spoon. Let cool to room temperature, cover, and refrigerate overnight.

In the Morning

■ Remove the chorizo from its casings and crumble the sausage into a heavy skillet. Set over medium heat and cook, stirring often, until the chorizo has rendered its fat and is lightly browned, 8 to 10 minutes. With a slotted spoon, transfer the chorizo to paper towels to drain.

■ Cut the chilled polenta into 6 equal squares. Cut each square in half on the diagonal. Set 2 large, heavy preferably nonstick skillets over medium heat. Divide the remaining 3 tablespoons olive oil between the skillets. When the oil is hot, add the polenta pieces to the skillets and cook, turning once or twice, until crisp and golden, 5 to 6 minutes per side.

■ Meanwhile, in a heavy saucepan over medium heat, combine the red chile sauce, chorizo, corn, and red wine. Bring to a simmer, then lower the heat and cook, stirring often, for 5 minutes.

■ Arrange 2 pieces of polenta on each of 6 plates. Spoon the chorizo sauce over the polenta, dividing it evenly and using it all. Garnish each serving with a sprig of cilantro, if desired, and serve immediately.

■■ Note: Mexican chorizo is a spicy, high-moisture sausage available in some Hispanic supermarkets. Firm, dry Spanish chorizo is not appropriate in this recipe. Hot Italian sausage can be substituted.

6 long green chiles (see Note, page 27)

¼ cup olive oil

6 cups cold water

2 cups coarse yellow cornmeal, preferably stoneground

Salt

1 pound Mexican chorizo (see Note)

3 cups Cafe Pasqual's Red Chile Sauce (page 70)

2 cups corn kernels (canned or thawed, frozen), well drained

½ cup dry red wine

6 fresh cilantro sprigs, for garnish (optional)

Chile Relleno Corn Casserole

Serves 4 as a main course, 8 as a side dish

Much less complicated than traditional individually fried chiles rellenos, this casserole of cheese-stuffed hot green chiles baked into a puffy corn custard makes a fine, rich side dish. It can also be served to four diners (two chiles each, then), as a main course, accompanied by the Watercress, Pink Grapefruit, and Avocado Salad on page 90. Masa, the instant cornmeal used for making tortillas (Quaker is the common brand) has a unique flavor, but regular cornmeal can be substituted.

8 large green chiles

Softened unsalted butter for the baking dish

7 eggs

1½ cups canned cream-style corn

1½ cups whipping cream

⅔ cup thinly sliced green onions

⅓ cup masa (treated corn tortilla meal) or yellow cornmeal, preferably stone-ground

1 teaspoon baking powder

¾ teaspoon salt

½ teaspoon freshly ground black pepper

½ pound jalapeño jack cheese or sharp Cheddar cheese, or a combination, cut into about sixteen 4 by-½-inch sticks

The Night Before

■ In the open flame of a gas burner or under a preheated broiler, roast the chiles, turning them occasionally, until the skins are lightly but evenly charred. Steam the chiles in a closed paper bag until cool. Rub away the burned skin. Cut a 2-inch slit in the stem end of each chile. With a finger, carefully scrape out as many seeds as possible without enlarging the slit any more than necessary. Wrap well and refrigerate.

In the Morning

■ Butter a 9-by-13-inch baking dish. Position a rack in the middle of the oven and preheat to 375 degrees F (350 degrees F if the baking dish is of glass).

■ In a large bowl, thoroughly whisk the eggs. Whisk in the creamed corn, cream, green onions, masa, baking powder, salt, and pepper. Stuff the chiles with the sticks of cheese, carefully slipping 2 sticks into each chile without tearing the chiles more than necessary. Arrange the chiles in a single layer crosswise in the prepared dish. Pour the egg mixture evenly over the chiles (it need not cover them completely). Bake until the custard is puffed, golden, and fairly firm when the dish is jiggled, 30 to 35 minutes.

■ Remove from the oven and let the casserole rest on a rack for 5 minutes. Serve hot.

Sausage, Pepper, and Potato Frittata Smothered with Green Salad
Serves 6

If quiche making daunts you due to pastry paranoia, consider the frittata. Slightly firmer than its French counterpart, but otherwise just as eggy and stuffed with assorted (mostly improvised) good things, the Italian frittata is baked, crustless, in a skillet, then, handsomely browned, is turned out onto a platter. Serve it hot or warm, and for taste, temperature, and textural contrast, top it with a big mound of tart, cool green salad.

The Night Before

■ In the open flame of a gas burner or under a preheated broiler, roast the peppers, turning them occasionally, until the skins are lightly but evenly charred. Steam the peppers in a closed paper bag until cool. Rub away the burned skins, stem and seed the peppers, and cut lengthwise into ¼-inch-wide strips. Wrap well and refrigerate.

■ Remove the sausage meat from the casings and crumble the meat into a large skillet. Set over medium heat and cook, breaking up the lumps with the edge of a spoon, until the meat is fully cooked and lightly browned, 8 to 10 minutes. With a slotted spoon, transfer the sausage to paper towels to drain. Let cool, wrap well, and refrigerate.

■ In a medium saucepan, cover the potato with cold water. Set over medium heat and bring to a boil. Lower the heat slightly, cover partially, and cook until just tender, about 30 minutes. Drain. Let cool, wrap well, and refrigerate.

In the Morning

■ Position a rack in the middle of the oven and preheat to 350 degrees F.

■ In a large bowl, thoroughly whisk the eggs. Whisk in the bread crumbs, cream, 1 teaspoon salt, and ¾ teaspoon pepper. Thinly slice the cooked potato. Stir the potato, pepper strips, and cooked sausage into the egg mixture.

■ Set a deep, preferably nonstick 10-inch skillet with an ovenproof handle over medium heat. Add the butter. When it foams, pour the egg mixture into the skillet. With a spoon, rearrange the sausage, peppers, and potato slices to distribute them evenly throughout the egg mixture. Set the skillet in the oven and bake until the edges of the frittata are puffed and lightly browned and the center is just set, 20 to 25 minutes.

■ Remove from the oven and let the frittata stand in the skillet on a rack for 10 minutes.

■ Meanwhile, in a large bowl, toss the salad greens with the olive oil. Season with a generous pinch of salt and toss again. Add 3 tablespoons of the vinegar and toss thoroughly. Taste and add the remaining vinegar if desired. The salad should be tart. Season generously with freshly ground pepper and toss again.

■ Invert a plate atop the skillet. Holding them together, flip the plate and skillet over; the frittata will drop onto the plate.

■ Cut the frittata into wedges. Set the wedges on plates. Top each wedge with a generous portion of salad, dividing it evenly and using it all. Serve immediately.

2 sweet peppers, preferably 1 red and 1 yellow
¾ pound (about 3 links) Italian sweet sausage with fennel seed
1 large red-skinned potato, about ½ pound
10 eggs
1 cup fresh bread crumbs
¾ cup whipping cream
Salt
Freshly ground black pepper
2 tablespoons (¼ stick) unsalted butter
12 cups mixed pungent salad greens (mesclun), rinsed and spun dry
⅓ cup olive oil
About ¼ cup red wine vinegar

Sherried Chicken Hash

Serves 6 to 8

This is luxurious hash-on-purpose, not hash frugally cobbled together from leftover roast chicken and gravy. The rich, moist, and tender results of that extra care will be readily evident in the empty condition of the plates that return to the kitchen. (Enterprising guests may also be found scraping the last of the crisp good stuff from around the edges of the baking dish.) Most of the several steps can be accomplished the night before.

3 **pounds boneless, skinless chicken breasts**

Salt

2 **bay leaves**

1¼ **pounds (about 4 medium) red-skinned potatoes, peeled and cut into ½-inch dice**

5 **tablespoons unsalted butter**

1 **large, heavy red sweet pepper, stemmed, cored, and cut into ¼-inch dice**

2 **leeks, white and tender green part only, finely chopped**

¼ **cup Amontillado sherry**

2 **tablespoons minced fresh thyme**

Velouté Sauce (recipe follows)

½ **cup coarse fresh bread crumbs**

The Night Before

■ Arrange the chicken breasts in a large, deep skillet that will just hold them in a single layer. Add cold water to cover. Evenly sprinkle in 2 teaspoons of salt and set over medium heat. Bring slowly to a simmer, turning the chicken breasts once. Continue to simmer until just cooked through, about 5 minutes (check the chicken breasts for doneness at their thickest point by piercing with a small knife). Remove the skillet from the heat and let the chicken cool to room temperature in the poaching liquid. With a slotted spoon, transfer the chicken to a cutting board and pat dry. Trim any fat or cartilage and cut the meat into ½-inch cubes.

■ In a saucepan, cover the potatoes with cold water. Stir in 2 teaspoons salt, set over medium heat, and bring to a boil. Cook the potatoes uncovered, stirring occasionally, until just tender, about 6 minutes. Drain immediately.

■ In a skillet over medium heat, melt 2 tablespoons of the butter. Add the sweet pepper and leeks. Cover and cook, stirring once or twice, for 10 minutes. Uncover, add the sherry, and raise the heat. Cook, stirring often, until the sherry is reduced to a glaze that just coats the vegetables, 2 to 3 minutes. Remove from the heat and stir in the thyme. Let cool.

■ In a large bowl, stir together the chicken, potatoes, glazed vegetable mixture, and Velouté Sauce. Cover and refrigerate.

In the Morning

■ Return the chicken mixture to room temperature. Position a rack in the upper third of the oven and preheat to 400 degrees F.

■ In a small saucepan over low heat, melt the remaining 3 tablespoons butter; remove from the heat. Spoon the chicken mixture into a shallow 2-quart baking dish (such as a 9-by-13-inch oval gratin dish) and spread it evenly with the back of a spoon. Sprinkle the top of the hash evenly with the bread crumbs. Drizzle the bread crumbs evenly with the melted butter.

■ Bake until the top of the hash is lightly browned and bubbling, about 40 minutes. Remove from the oven and let the hash stand on a rack for 5 minutes. Serve hot.

Velouté Sauce

Makes about 3½ cups

- In a heavy saucepan over low heat, melt the butter. Whisk in the flour and cook without browning, stirring occasionally, for 5 minutes.
- Remove from the heat and gradually whisk in the stock. Return the pan to low heat and whisk in the salt, pepper, and nutmeg. Cover partially and cook, stirring often, until the sauce is thick and glossy, about 20 minutes. Remove from the heat and let cool to room temperature.

6 tablespoons (¾ stick) unsalted butter

½ cup unbleached all-purpose flour

3 cups chicken stock or reduced-sodium canned chicken broth

¾ teaspoon salt

½ teaspoon freshly ground black pepper

Pinch of freshly grated nutmeg

Devilled Shrimp

Serves 8

Inspiration for this dish comes from the South, where shrimp are abundant, affordable, admired, and frequently served up broiled, under a gloss of piquant butter. To make the dish special (and to make it less likely that the broiling will dry the shellfish out), select jumbo (12 or so to the pound) shrimp. Spoon them and their delicious pan juices over the cheese grits on page 58.

The Night Before

- In a bowl, with the back of a spoon, mash together thoroughly the butter, anchovy fillets, garlic, mustard, pepper sauce, Worcestershire sauce, and salt. Cover and refrigerate.

In the Morning

- Bring the butter mixture just to room temperature.
- Preheat the broiler. Arrange the shrimp in a single, close-fitting layer in a broilerproof serving dish. Smear the butter evenly over the shrimp.
- Broil the shrimp without turning them until they are lightly browned on top and just cooked through, 5 to 6 minutes. Sprinkle with the parsley and serve immediately.

8 tablespoons (1 stick) unsalted butter, softened

4 oil-packed anchovy fillets, drained and minced

2 garlic cloves, forced through a press

1½ teaspoons green-peppercorn mustard

1½ teaspoons hot-pepper sauce such as Tabasco

1½ teaspoons Worcestershire sauce

¼ teaspoon salt

2 pounds (about 24) jumbo shrimp, shelled and deveined, with tails left intact

¼ cup minced fresh flat-leaf parsley

Orange-and-Madeira-Glazed Ham with Raisin Sauce

Serves 12 with leftovers

An enormous, beautifully glazed ham is the best brunch centerpiece I know, signaling good times and smoky abundance ahead to all who see it. Little effort is required—mainly, buy a good, nonsupermarket ham and do as little as possible to it—which frees time for the cook to spend on a whole crowd of ham-friendly accompaniments. (The other bonus is plenty of leftovers for the coming week of breakfasts, lunches, and suppers.) Dried pitted tart cherries can replace the raisins in the sauce.

1 fully cooked, bone-in, brine-cured smoked ham, about 16 pounds, at room temperature

2 cups water

4 cups chicken stock or canned low-sodium broth

1½ cups medium-dry Madeira wine

2 bay leaves

⅔ cup dark raisins

⅔ cup golden raisins

1 can (6 ounces) frozen orange juice concentrate, thawed

About 36 whole cloves

1 tablespoon cornstarch

Salt

Freshly ground black pepper

- Position a rack in the lower third of the oven and preheat to 325 degrees F.
- If there is a tough rind on the upper side of the ham, cut it away. Trim away any fat beneath the rind to a thickness of no more than ¼ inch. With a long, sharp knife, score a shallow diamond pattern into the top of the ham. Set the ham in a shallow roasting pan. Add the water to the pan. Set the ham in the oven and bake for 2 hours.
- Meanwhile, in a saucepan over medium heat, bring the stock, ½ cup of the Madeira, and the bay leaves just to a boil. In a heatproof bowl, place the dark and golden raisins. Pour the hot stock mixture over the raisins and let stand, stirring once or twice, until the stock is cool and the raisins have plumped.
- In a bowl, stir together the remaining 1 cup Madeira and the orange juice concentrate. Remove the ham from the oven and pour off the water from the roasting pan. Insert a clove into the center of each scored diamond. Return the ham to the oven and baste with one-fourth of the Madeira mixture. Bake for 10 minutes. Repeat until the basting mixture is used up and the ham is shiny and golden, about 30 minutes. Remove from the oven and let the ham rest in the roasting pan on a rack for at least 20 minutes.
- Meanwhile, strain the stock mixture into a saucepan, reserving the raisins and bay leaves. Measure out ¼ cup of the stock and pour it over the cornstarch in a small bowl; stir until smooth. Add the bay leaves to the remaining stock in the saucepan and set over medium heat. Bring to a brisk simmer and cook uncovered until reduced by one-third, 8 to 10 minutes. Discard the bay leaves. Stir the cornstarch mixture again to blend, then stir it and the reserved raisins into the sauce. Lower the heat and simmer gently, stirring often, until the sauce turns clear and thickens, about 1 minute. Add salt to taste and season generously with pepper.
- Carve the ham and serve it hot or warm, passing the raisin sauce separately.

Grill-Smoked Salmon Fillets with Maple-Corn Relish

Serves 6

It is a sign of the changing times when the grill gets lighted even at brunch. The light, colorful, and zesty food that results seems naturally celebratory, and the casual outdoor atmosphere suits the more laid-back style of entertaining that brunch defines. Chips of apple or hickory wood flavor the salmon rather heavily with their especially pungent smoke—an important contrast to the colorful, spicy, and slightly sweet corn relish that is spooned over the fillets as they come off the grill.

The Night Before

- In the open flame of a gas burner or under a preheated broiler, roast the sweet pepper, turning it, until the skin is lightly but evenly charred. Steam the pepper in a closed paper bag until cool. Rub away the burned skin, stem and seed the pepper, and chop into ¼-inch pieces.
- In a bowl, stir together the roasted pepper, corn, maple syrup, corn oil, cider vinegar, pepper sauce, turmeric, and ¼ teaspoon salt. Cover and refrigerate.

In the Morning

- If using a charcoal grill or a gas grill with lava rocks, soak the wood chips in water to cover for at least 30 minutes. Add the green onions to the corn relish and let it come to room temperature.
- Light a charcoal fire and let it burn down until the coals are evenly white, or preheat a gas grill (medium-high). Drain the wood chips if you have soaked them and scatter them over the coals or firestones (or follow the manufacturer's directions for using unsoaked chips in a grill with a smoking compartment). Lightly oil the rack. When the chips are smoking heavily, position the rack about 6 inches above the heat source. Lay the fillets on the rack, skin side down, cover, and grill for 4 minutes. Turn the fillets and grill another 3 to 4 minutes, or until done to your liking.
- Immediately transfer the fillets to plates. Season lightly to taste with salt and pepper. Spoon the corn relish and any juices in the bowl over the fillets, dividing it evenly and using it all. Serve immediately.

1 red sweet pepper

1 package (10 ounces) frozen corn kernels, thawed and well drained

2 tablespoons maple syrup

2 tablespoons corn oil, plus oil for grilling the fillets

5 teaspoons cider vinegar

1½ teaspoons hot-pepper sauce, such as Tabasco

¾ teaspoon ground turmeric

Salt

2 cups apple or hickory wood chips

⅓ cup thinly sliced green onions

6 salmon fillets, about 2¼ pounds total and each about 1 inch thick

Freshly ground black pepper

Chili-Rubbed Brunch Steaks with Red Pepper Sauce

Serves 4

Team these grilled, chili-rubbed rib eyes with the Chile Relleno Corn Casserole on page 102 and you have a new suitable-for-company version of classic steak and eggs.

The Night Before

- In the open flame of a gas burner or under a preheated broiler, roast the pepper, turning it, until the skin is lightly but evenly charred. Steam the pepper in a closed paper bag until cool. Rub away the burned skin, stem and seed the pepper, and chop.
- In a small food processor, combine the roasted pepper, sour cream, vinegar, pepper sauce, and ¼ teaspoon of the salt, and process until smooth. Transfer to a small bowl, cover, and refrigerate.

In the Morning

- If using a charcoal grill or a gas grill with lava rocks, soak the wood chips in water to cover for at least 30 minutes. In a small bowl, stir together the chili powder and brown sugar. Rub the chile mixture well into both sides of each steak. Lay the steaks on a plate, cover, and let stand at room temperature for 30 minutes. Bring the red pepper sauce to room temperature.
- Light a charcoal fire and let it burn down until the coals are evenly white, or preheat a gas grill (medium-high). Drain the wood chips if you have soaked them and scatter them over the coals or firestones (or follow the manufacturer's directions for using unsoaked chips in a grill with a smoking compartment). When the chips are smoking heavily, position the rack about 6 inches above the heat source. Lay the steaks on the rack, cover, and grill for 4 minutes. Turn the steaks, cover, and grill for another 3 to 4 minutes for fairly rare, or until done to your liking.
- Transfer the steaks to plates. Season lightly with salt. Drizzle the red pepper sauce over them, dividing it evenly and using it all. Serve immediately.

1 red sweet pepper
2 tablespoons sour cream
½ teaspoon balsamic vinegar
½ teaspoon hot-pepper sauce such as Tabasco
Salt
2 cups hickory wood chips
4 teaspoons chili powder
2 teaspoons granulated brown sugar
4 rib eye steaks, about 2 pounds total and each ½ inch thick

SIDES AND BREADS

4

Maple-Butternut Squash Purée

Serves 4

Not only is this brilliant gold purée easy (it can be done entirely in advance), but its sweet touch of maple links it to many of the rich, smoky flavors that are the hallmark of a good brunch.

2 medium-large butternut squashes, about 3½ pounds total, halved and seeds and fibers scooped out

4 tablespoons (½ stick) unsalted butter

½ cup finely chopped yellow onions

¼ teaspoon freshly grated nutmeg

½ cup chicken stock

⅓ cup maple syrup

½ teaspoon salt

½ teaspoon freshly ground black pepper

The Night Before

- Position a rack in the middle of the oven and preheat to 400 degrees F.
- Set the squash halves, cut sides up, on a baking sheet. Bake until the squash halves, pierced at their thickest, are very tender, about 45 minutes. Remove from the oven and let cool slightly. When the squash can just be comfortably handled, scoop and scrape the flesh (including any browned edges) out of the skins into a food processor.
- Meanwhile, in a small skillet over low heat, melt the butter. Add the onions and nutmeg and cook uncovered, stirring occasionally, until the onions are lightly colored and tender, about 10 minutes. Transfer to the food processor. Add the stock, maple syrup, salt, and pepper, and process, stopping several times to scrape down the sides of the work bowl, until smooth. Adjust the seasoning. Let cool completely, then cover tightly and refrigerate.

In the Morning

- In a heavy saucepan over low heat, warm the purée, stirring often to prevent scorching, until heated through and steaming, 5 to 7 minutes. Serve hot.

Pumpkin Spoon Bread

Serves 4 to 6

Falling somewhere between a cornmeal soufflé and a savory pumpkin pudding, this soft, tender, quick-to-assemble side dish is especially wonderful alongside ham, bacon, or other smoked meats. It also goes well with plainer egg dishes. Good as it comes from the dish, it's even better with a dollop of butter and a generous grinding of black pepper.

- Position a rack in the middle of the oven and preheat to 375 degrees F. Put the butter in a 6-cup soufflé dish and place in the oven to melt.
- Meanwhile, in a large bowl, whisk together the pumpkin, sugar, paprika, and salt. One at a time, whisk in the eggs. Whisk in the buttermilk. Add the cornmeal, baking powder, and baking soda and mix well.
- Tilt the soufflé dish to coat the sides with the melted butter. Pour the pumpkin mixture into the dish. Set the dish in the oven and bake until puffed and light brown, about 40 minutes. Serve immediately.

3 tablespoons unsalted butter

I can (16 ounces) unsweetened solid-pack pumpkin purée (not pie filling)

7 tablespoons sugar

I tablespoon Hungarian sweet paprika

I teaspoon salt

4 eggs, at room temperature

⅓ cup buttermilk, at room temperature

I cup coarse yellow cornmeal, preferably stoneground

I teaspoon baking powder

½ teaspoon baking soda

Stilton Potato Gratin

Serves 6

One of the two or three greatest cheeses of the world, real English farmhouse Stilton, with its combined flavors of blue cheese and Cheddar, transforms perfectly delicious potatoes gratin into something extraordinary. Serve these alongside the glazed ham on page 106, or try them as an unusual accompaniment to scrambled eggs or omelets.

- Position a rack in the middle of the oven and preheat to 350 degrees F. Butter a shallow 2-quart baking dish (such as a 9-by-13-inch oval gratin dish).
- Arrange about one-third of the potato slices evenly in the baking dish. Scatter half the cheese evenly over the potatoes and season to taste with pepper. Arrange about half the remaining potatoes evenly over the cheese; scatter the remaining cheese over the potato layer and season with pepper. Arrange the remaining potatoes evenly over the cheese. Pour the chicken stock over the potatoes. Dot the top of the gratin with the butter and season with pepper.
- Bake the potatoes, tilting the pan occasionally to baste the potatoes with the liquid, until the top of the gratin is lightly browned, the potatoes are tender, and the sauce has thickened, 1 hour and 10 to 15 minutes.
- Remove from the oven and let the gratin rest on a rack for 5 minutes before serving.

2½ pounds (about 5 medium) russet (baking) potatoes, peeled and thinly sliced crosswise

½ pound Stilton cheese, rind trimmed, crumbled

Freshly ground black pepper

1⅓ cups chicken stock or reduced-sodium canned chicken broth

2 tablespoons unsalted butter, cut into small pieces

Orange Beets

Serves 4

Baking the beets, rather than boiling them, intensifies their color and flavor.

**1½ pounds (about 7) small beets,
trimmed but not peeled
1 cup plus 1 tablespoon fresh
orange juice, strained
2½ tablespoons sugar
2 tablespoons unsalted butter
2 teaspoons red wine vinegar
1 tablespoon minced orange zest
(colored peel)
½ teaspoon salt
¼ teaspoon pepper
2 teaspoons cornstarch**

The Night Before

- Position a rack in the middle of the oven and preheat to 400 degrees F.
- Tightly wrap the beets in 2 aluminum foil packets. Set the packets on a baking sheet and bake the beets until they are just barely cooked through, about 50 minutes. Let cool in the packets to room temperature. Peel the beets. Wrap well and refrigerate.

In the Morning

- Cut the beets into eighths. In a nonreactive saucepan over medium heat, combine the beets, the 1 cup orange juice, the sugar, butter, vinegar, orange zest, salt, and pepper. Bring to a brisk simmer and cook uncovered, stirring occasionally, until the sauce is reduced, about 10 minutes.
- Meanwhile, in a small bowl, stir the remaining 1 tablespoon orange juice into the cornstarch until smooth. Lower the heat under the beets. Stir in the cornstarch mixture and simmer gently until the sauce has thickened slightly, about 1 minute.

Brunch Bread

Serves 6 to 8

This rich and rather gooey cheese-meat-and-bread creation is designed to add a little something extra to the brunch plate, particularly when there is no meat (or at least red meat) elsewhere on the menu. Although I call for Gouda and pastrami, I only mean to indicate that this eccentric pairing worked for me. Ham, corned beef, even smoked turkey can be substituted, and any cheese that melts is worth a try. Start with good bread, and it's hard to go wrong.

**1 long loaf crusty bread, preferably
sourdough, 12 inches long, split
lengthwise
3 tablespoons unsalted butter,
softened
6 ounces pastrami, thinly sliced
½ pound Gouda cheese, rind
trimmed and thinly sliced**

- Position a rack in the middle of the oven and preheat to 375 degrees F.
- Spread the cut sides of the bread halves evenly with the butter. Arrange the meat evenly over the bottom half of the loaf. Lay half the cheese evenly over the meat. Set the top of the bread loaf in place. With a long serrated knife, cut the loaf crosswise into 8 equal pieces.
- Carefully transfer the loaf to a large piece of aluminum foil, reassembling it if necessary. Wrap tightly and bake for 15 minutes. Open the top of the foil packet. Evenly lay the remaining cheese over the top of the loaf. Return the loaf to the oven and bake until the cheese on top is melted and lightly browned, another 15 to 20 minutes.
- Remove the loaf from the foil and transfer to a cutting board. Serve on the board, letting guests pull the loaf apart as they serve themselves.

Wild Rice and Wild Mushrooms

Serves 4

For this easy but delicious side dish, look for French or Italian dried mushrooms (cèpes and porcini respectively; American specimens are somewhat milder in taste) and extra-fancy, hand-harvested (not paddy-grown) wild rice.

The Night Before

■ Bring a saucepan three-fourths full of water to a boil. Stir in the wild rice, 2 teaspoons salt, and the bay leaf. Cover partially and cook briskly, stirring occasionally, until the rice is almost tender and the ends of the rice are beginning to burst, about 45 minutes. Drain. Discard the bay leaf. Let cool, cover, and refrigerate.

In the Morning

■ In a small saucepan over medium heat, bring the stock to a simmer. Add the cèpes, remove the pan from the heat, and let stand, covered, stirring once or twice, until cool. With a slotted spoon, remove the cèpes from the liquid. Mince them. Pour off and reserve the clear portion of the liquid and discard any sandy residue.

■ In a medium-large skillet over low heat, melt the butter. Add the minced cèpes, onions, carrots, garlic, marjoram, and thyme. Cover and cook, stirring once or twice, for 5 minutes. Add the fresh mushrooms, season with ¼ teaspoon salt, and cook covered, stirring once or twice, until they begin to render their juices, about 5 minutes. Stir in the wild rice, the reserved mushroom soaking liquid, and ½ teaspoon pepper. Cover and cook, stirring occasionally, until the rice has absorbed almost, but not all, of the liquid, about 10 minutes.

■ Adjust the seasoning, stir in the parsley, and serve immediately.

¾ cup wild rice, rinsed
Salt
1 bay leaf
1 cup chicken stock
½ ounce (generous ½ cup) dried cèpe or porcini mushrooms, rinsed
4 tablespoons (½ stick) unsalted butter
½ cup finely chopped yellow onions
⅓ cup finely chopped carrots
1 garlic clove, minced
½ teaspoon dried marjoram, crumbled
¼ teaspoon dried thyme, crumbled
5 ounces (about 6 medium) fresh brown (cremini) mushrooms, wiped clean and thinly sliced
Freshly ground black pepper
¼ cup minced fresh flat-leaf parsley

Easy Cherry-Cheese Strudel
Serves 6

Strudel dough (or filo leaves) can be found frozen in gourmet shops and some supermarkets, or purchased fresh from Greek bakeries in large cities. The dough sheets look impossibly thin, but are actually very forgiving (and certainly loads less work than rolling and stretching strudel dough from scratch). The following kirsch-spiked cheese strudel, studded with dried cherries, is rich but only slightly sweet, and is so impressive a brunch pastry, guests will be certain you have Viennese ancestors.

½ **pound small-curd cream-style cottage cheese**

2 **eggs**

⅓ **cup dried pitted tart cherries**

2 **ounces low-fat farmer cheese, shredded**

½ **cup plus 4 teaspoons fine dried bread crumbs**

3 **tablespoons sugar**

2 **tablespoons kirsch (unsweetened cherry brandy) (optional)**

6 **tablespoons (¾ stick) unsalted butter, melted**

Filo dough, fresh or thawed (see Note)

Confectioners' sugar, in a sieve

The Night Before
■ Force the cottage cheese through a sieve into a bowl. Stir in the eggs, cherries, farmer cheese, the ¼ cup bread crumbs, sugar, and kirsch. Cover and refrigerate.

In the Morning
■ Position a rack in the middle of the oven and preheat to 400 degrees F. Lightly brush a baking sheet with some of the melted butter.

■ Moisten a clean towel with water and wring out the excess. Unwrap the filo dough. Lay 1 sheet of filo, short side toward you, on a work surface; cover the remaining filo with the dampened towel. Lightly brush the filo sheet with melted butter. Evenly sprinkle 1 teaspoon of the remaining bread crumbs over the filo. Lay a second filo sheet over the first, again covering the remaining sheets with the towel. Lightly butter the second filo sheet and then evenly sprinkle it with 1 teaspoon of bread crumbs. Lay a third filo sheet over the second. Cover the unused filo dough with the towel. Lightly brush the third filo sheet with butter and evenly sprinkle it with half the remaining bread crumbs. Repeat with 1 more sheet of filo, brushing it with butter and sprinkling it with the remaining bread crumbs.

■ Spoon the chilled cheese filling in a thick band across the short side of the stack of filo sheets closest to you, leaving a 2-inch border on 3 sides. Fold both long sides of the filo over the filling, then roll the filo up over the filling from the short side closest to you to form a log-shaped packet. Carefully transfer the strudel to the prepared baking sheet. Brush with half the remaining melted butter.

■ Set the sheet pan in the oven and bake for 15 minutes. Lower the heat to 350 degrees F, brush the strudel with the remaining butter and bake until crisp and brown, another 15 to 20 minutes.

■ Remove from the oven and cool the strudel on the pan on a rack for 10 minutes. Transfer to a work surface. With a serrated knife, carefully cut the strudel into 1½ inch slices. Transfer to a serving platter. Dust the strudel with the confectioners' sugar. Serve warm.

■■ Note: Bring fresh filo to room temperature before using. Let frozen filo thaw in the package in the refrigerator for 48 hours. Bring it to room temperature before using. Draping the filo with a dampened towel helps keep it from cracking. Well-wrapped filo can be refrigerated for several days. Fresh filo can be frozen, but thawed filo does not successfully refreeze.

Jumbo Ham, Corn, and Red Pepper Muffins

Makes 4 muffins

These oversized, jam-packed muffins are actually the main course, needing only eggs, potatoes, and fruit to round out the menu. The extra-large pan called for is sometimes sold as a "Texas muffin" tin and can be found in some well-stocked cookware shops or ordered from a good catalog. The cups should hold about one-half cup.

The Night Before
- In the open flame of a gas burner or under a preheated broiler, roast the pepper, turning it occasionally, until the skin is lightly but evenly charred. Steam the pepper in a closed paper bag until cool. Rub away the burned skin, stem and seed the pepper, and then chop. Wrap well and refrigerate.

In the Morning
- Position a rack in the middle of the oven and preheat to 400 degrees F. Spray 4 cups of a jumbo muffin tin well with nonstick spray.
- Into a large bowl, sift together twice the flour, cornmeal, sugar, baking powder, and salt. In a smaller bowl whisk the egg. Whisk in the buttermilk and the melted butter. Add the egg mixture to the dry ingredients and stir until almost combined. Add the ham, red pepper, and corn and stir until just combined; do not overmix. Spoon the batter into the prepared muffin cups, dividing it evenly and mounding it slightly.
- Bake the muffins until they are puffed and golden brown and a tester inserted into the center of a muffin comes out clean, 25 to 30 minutes.
- Remove from the oven and cool the muffins in the pan on a rack for 5 minutes. Carefully run a knife around the edge of each muffin cup and gently remove the muffins. Serve hot or warm, accompanied with butter, if desired.

1 red sweet pepper
Nonstick spray, for the muffin tin
1 cup unbleached all-purpose flour
1 cup coarse yellow cornmeal, preferably stoneground
⅓ cup sugar
1 tablespoon baking powder
½ teaspoon salt
1 egg
⅔ cup buttermilk, at room temperature
6 tablespoons (¾ stick) unsalted butter, melted and cooled slightly, plus butter for serving (optional)
5 ounces firm, smoky baked ham, cut into ½-inch cubes
¾ cup corn kernels (canned or thawed, frozen), well drained

Blueberry Crumb Buns

Makes 20 buns

These old-fashioned, streusel-topped crumb buns are adapted from a recipe by Richard Sax, which was in turn adapted from The Rock Hill Bakehouse in Gansevoort, New York. This explains the rather large yield, but trust me, twenty buns does not mean you will need a crowd that large to dispose of these rich, cinnamony treats. The dough, as benefits its professional origins, is rather stiff and hard to handle (a heavy-duty electric stand mixer is almost a requirement), but most of the work gets done the night before.

Dough

- **2 packages (2½ teaspoons each) active dry yeast**
- **3 tablespoons warm (105 to 115 degrees F) water**
- **1 tablespoon plus ¼ cup granulated sugar**
- **½ pound (2 sticks) chilled unsalted butter**
- **4 cups unbleached all-purpose flour (see Note), plus flour for the work surface**
- **¾ cup sour cream**
- **3 egg yolks**
- **4 teaspoons finely minced orange zest (colored peel)**
- **1½ teaspoons salt**
- **1 tablespoon canola or other flavorless oil**

The Night Before

■ For the dough, in the bowl of a heavy-duty stand mixer, or in a large mixing bowl, stir together the yeast, water, and the 1 tablespoon granulated sugar. Let stand until foamy, about 5 minutes.

■ Meanwhile, loosely wrap the butter in a large sheet of plastic wrap. Beat the butter, using a rolling pin as a bat, until it is malleable but still cold; set aside.

■ Add the ¼ cup granulated sugar, the flour, sour cream, egg yolks, orange zest, and salt. Using the mixer fitted with a dough hook (or by hand with a wooden spoon), mix on low speed to blend; raise the speed to high and mix until well blended, several minutes. Gradually add the butter and beat to form a stiff dough. Beat, stopping occasionally to scrape down the sides of the bowl, for 6 minutes. Lightly flour a work surface.

■ Turn out the dough and knead until it becomes slightly more elastic, 2 to 3 minutes. Shape into a ball. Oil a large bowl with the corn oil. Add the ball of dough, turn to coat it with the oil, and cover the bowl tightly with plastic wrap. Refrigerate overnight.

■ For the streusel, in a food processor, combine the flour, sugar, and cinnamon and pulse to blend. With the motor running, dribble in the vanilla. Add the butter and process until large lumps resembling a rather messy cookie dough form. Transfer to a bowl, cover tightly with plastic wrap, and refrigerate overnight.

In the Morning

■ Line the bottom of an 18-by-12-inch jelly-roll pan with parchment or waxed paper; butter the paper and the sides of the pan.

■ Turn out the dough onto a lightly floured work surface. It will be cold and stiff. Using a rolling pin, begin working and rolling the dough out to a rectangle approximately the same size as the jelly roll pan. Transfer the dough to the pan. Pat it out evenly to fill the pan to its edges; patch any tears by pressing with your fingers. With a pizza wheel or a sharp knife, cut the dough into 20 rectangles. Cover the pan tightly with plastic wrap and let the dough rise in a warm place until doubled, about 3 hours.

■ Position a rack in the middle of the oven and preheat to 350 degrees F. Uncover the dough and scatter the blueberries evenly over it, pressing them lightly into the dough to hold them in place. Crumble the chilled streusel with a fork into pieces about twice the size of peas. Scatter the streusel evenly over the dough, using it all.

■ Set the pan in the oven and bake the crumb buns until the streusel is lightly browned and the edges of the dough are golden, 30 to 35 minutes; do not overbake.

■ Remove from the oven and let stand in the pan on a rack for 5 minutes. Sift the confectioners' sugar lightly over the crumb buns (the streusel should still show through). Serve warm.

■■ Note: To measure the flour, stir it in the canister with a fork to lighten, then spoon it into a dry-measure cup and sweep level.

Streusel

1⅓ cup unbleached all-purpose flour
⅔ cup sugar
2½ teaspoons ground cinnamon
1 teaspoon vanilla extract
11 tablespoons chilled unsalted butter, cut into small pieces
Softened unsalted butter, for the jellyroll pan
2 cups blueberries, picked over, or 2 cups unthawed, frozen blueberries
Confectioners' sugar, in a sieve

DESSERTS

5

Deep-Dish Raspberry and Black Cherry Pie—page 129

St. Louie Ooey-Gooey Berry Butter Cake

Serves 8

This buttery cake, with its cheesecakelike topping and baked-on garnish of fresh berries, is the specialty of Renee Studt Scott, head breakfast cook at The Sylvia Beach Hotel in Newport, Oregon. It is not quite as rich as its wonderful title would indicate, but then it's not spa fare either, and it goes together with a welcome lack of kitchen fuss.

Room-temperature unsalted butter for the baking pan, plus 5 tablespoons unsalted butter, melted

Flour for the baking pan, plus 1 cup unbleached allpurpose flour (see Note)

½ teaspoon baking powder

½ teaspoon baking soda

¼ teaspoon salt

½ cup granulated sugar

2 eggs

⅔ cup sour cream

½ teaspoon vanilla extract

1½ cups confectioners' sugar

½ pound cream cheese, at room temperature

2 tablespoons fresh lemon juice

2 cups berries (mix at least two types) such as blackberries, Marion berries, raspberries, boysenberries or blueberries

■ Position a rack in the middle of the oven and preheat to 350 degrees F. Butter a 9-inch cake pan with a removable bottom (or use a 9-inch springform pan). Flour the pan and tap out the excess.

■ Into a bowl, sift together twice the flour, baking powder, baking soda, and salt. In another bowl, with an electric mixer set on medium speed, cream together the melted butter, granulated sugar, and 1 of the eggs until pale and thickened, about 1 minute. Beat in the sour cream and vanilla. Add the dry ingredients and beat until smooth.

■ Spread the batter evenly in the prepared pan. Bake until the cake has risen and is golden and springs back when gently pressed, about 20 minutes.

■ Meanwhile, in a bowl, with an electric mixer set on medium speed, beat together the confectioners' sugar, cream cheese, the remaining egg, and the lemon juice until smooth. Remove the cake from the oven and pour the cream cheese mixture onto the hot cake, spreading it evenly to the edges. Scatter the berries evenly over the cream cheese mixture.

■ Return the cake to the oven and bake until the edges of the topping are set and lightly browned but the center still jiggles when the pan is shaken, about 25 minutes.

■ Remove from the oven and let the cake cool in the pan on a rack to room temperature. Run the tip of a knife around the sides of the cake to loosen it from the pan and then push it free from the sides (or release the sides of a springform pan). With a long, thin knife, carefully slide if off the pan bottom onto a serving plate and serve at room temperature.

■■ Note: To measure the flour, stir it in the canister with a fork to lighten, then spoon into a dry-measure cup and sweep level.

Panna Cotta with Crushed Raspberry Sauce

Serves 4

Panna cotta means "cooked cream" in Italian, and indeed, that is just about all this simple but elegant little dessert consists of. If you have ever had the English nursery sweet known as junket, you'll be amazed at the transforming power of an Italian name and a splash of hazelnut liqueur.

Nonstick spray
2 **tablespoons plus ½ cup milk**
¼ **cup Frangelico or other hazelnut liqueur**
1 **package (2¼ teaspoons) unflavored gelatin**
1½ **cups whipping cream**
¼ **cup plus 2 tablespoons sugar**
Pinch of salt
9 **ounces (2¼ cups) raspberries, picked over**

The Night Before

- Lightly coat four ½-cup ramekins with nonstick spray.
- In a small bowl, combine the 2 tablespoons milk and 2 tablespoons of the liqueur. Sprinkle the gelatin over the liquid and let stand for about 10 minutes, or until completely softened.
- Meanwhile, in a small saucepan, combine the remaining ½ cup milk, the cream, the ¼ cup sugar, and the salt. Set over medium heat and bring just to a simmer. Remove from the heat and stir in the softened gelatin mixture. Whisk until smooth. Divide the milk mixture among the prepared ramekins. Let cool, cover, and refrigerate. The desserts will be jiggly.

In the Morning

- In a small bowl, partially crush the raspberries with a fork. Stir in the remaining 2 tablespoons liqueur and the remaining 2 tablespoons sugar and let stand for 30 minutes.
- One at a time, dip the ramekins into hot water, then run a sharp, thin-bladed knife around the rim. Invert each ramekin onto a dessert plate; the desserts will drop out. Spoon the sauce partially over and around each dessert and serve immediately.

Marie Simmons's Dark Gingerbread

Makes one 10-inch cake; serves 12

If you, like I, have long sought the perfect dark, moist, and spicy gingerbread, this has to be the one. (It looks great, too, baked in a bundt instead of a flat little pan, making it the perfect dramatic brunch centerpiece.) Except for the addition of cardamom (which is my own personal gingerbread secret ingredient), it comes unchanged from Richard Sax's *Classic Home Desserts*. Though it may not cut neatly, serve the cake slightly warm, and accompany it with either of the sauces suggested below.

1 tablespoon unsalted butter, melted, plus ½ pound (2 sticks) unsalted butter, at room temperature

Flour for the bundt pan, plus 3½ cups unbleached all-purpose flour (see Note)

2 tablespoons ground ginger

2 teaspoons ground cardamom

2 teaspoons baking soda

½ teaspoon ground cloves

½ teaspoon salt

¼ cup minced crystallized ginger

1 cup packed dark brown sugar

2 eggs

2 cups unsulphured molasses

1 cup boiling water

Lemon Slice Sauce (page 125); Ginger-Pear Compote (page 74), heated to a simmer; or unsweetened whipped cream, for serving (optional)

- Position a rack in the middle of the oven and preheat to 350 degrees F. Brush the inside of a 10-inch bundt pan with the melted butter; sprinkle with a fine coating of flour and shake out the excess.
- Into a medium bowl, sift together twice the 3½ cups flour, ground ginger, cardamom, baking soda, cloves, and salt. Stir in the crystallized ginger.
- In a large bowl, beat the 2 sticks butter with an electric mixer set at medium-high speed until light and fluffy, 2 or 3 minutes. Add the sugar and beat until smooth. Beat in the eggs, one at a time, beating well after each addition. Gradually add the molasses in a slow, steady stream, beating until blended.
- Gradually beat the dry ingredients into the batter just until blended, no longer; turn off the mixer. Add the boiling water to the batter, ⅓ cup at a time, stirring gently but thoroughly by hand with a large rubber spatula after each addition. Spoon the batter into the prepared pan.
- Bake until the cake just pulls away from the sides of the pan, about 55 minutes. Remove from the oven and let the gingerbread cool in the pan on a rack until warm, about 20 minutes. The top of the cake may sink slightly upon cooling.
- Run the tip of a knife around the sides of the cake to loosen it from the pan. Invert the cake onto a platter. Serve, if desired, with one of the suggested accompaniments.
- ■ Note: To measure the flour, stir it in the canister with a fork to lighten, then spoon into dry-measure cups and sweep level.

Lemon Slice Sauce

Makes about 2⅔ cups

- In a nonreactive saucepan, stir together the sugar and cornstarch. Gradually whisk in the cider; stir until smooth.
- Set the pan over medium heat and bring the mixture to a boil. Stir in the lemon juice, zest, lemon slices, butter, and salt. Cook just until the butter melts, about 2 minutes. Serve immediately.

1 cup sugar

2 tablespoons cornstarch

1 cup apple cider

½ cup fresh lemon juice

Finely grated zest (colored peel) of 2 large lemons

2 large lemons, thinly sliced, then slices quartered

4 tablespoons (½ stick) unsalted butter

¼ teaspoon salt

Maple-Sweetened Buckwheat Plum Clafouti

Serves 6 to 8

Sharp eyes will recognize that this simple country sweet is merely fruit baked in a thin pancake batter. Unlike the traditional French clafouti, made with cherries and served only as dessert, this buckwheat-maple version is good at brunch and breakfast as well, served with eggs and ham or bacon. Offer it warm, sprinkled with confectioners' sugar.

- In a bowl, combine the plums and maple syrup and let stand for 30 minutes.
- Position a rack in the middle of the oven and preheat to 350 degrees F. Generously butter a shallow, 2-quart baking dish (such as a 9-by-13inch oval gratin dish).
- Drain the plums in a sieve set over a bowl. In a food processor, combine the plum juices, half-and-half, sugar, eggs, vanilla, unbleached flour, and buckwheat flour. Process until smooth; the batter will be thin.
- Pour half the batter into the prepared pan. Set it in the oven and bake until the batter just begins to set, 5 to 7 minutes. Spread the chunks of plum over the set batter (and pour over any additional juices that may have collected in the bowl), then pour in the remaining batter. Bake the clafouti until it is puffed, the edges are lightly browned, and a tester inserted into the center comes out clean, about 1 hour.
- Remove from the oven and let the clafouti rest on a rack for about 15 minutes. Sprinkle heavily with confectioners' sugar and serve warm.

1¼ pounds red plums such as Santa Rosa, pitted and cut into ½-inch chunks

½ cup maple syrup

Room-temperature unsalted butter, for the baking dish

¾ cup half-and-half

¼ cup sugar

3 eggs

2 teaspoons vanilla extract

⅓ cup unbleached all-purpose flour

⅓ cup buckwheat flour, preferably stone-ground

Confectioners' sugar, in a sieve

Country Pear and Almond Tart

Makes one 10-inch tart; serves 8

This fruit-and-custard tart has simple country flavors—just right for starting the day. As is usual with such French-inspired creations, the recipe is lengthy, but several of the steps can be accomplished well in advance.

3 **cups dry white wine**

1⅓ **cups sugar**

¼ **cup fresh lemon juice**

8 **strips lemon zest (colored peel), each 3 inches long by ½ inch wide**

1 **vanilla bean, split lengthwise**

6 **firm but ripe Anjou pears, about 3 pounds total, peeled, halved, and cored**

3 **tablespoons sliced unblanched almonds**

Baked Tart Shell (recipe follows)

½ **cup crabapple jelly**

3 **eggs**

3 **tablespoons unbleached all-purpose flour**

¾ **teaspoon baking powder**

½ **teaspoon vanilla extract**

¼ **teaspoon salt**

⅛ **teaspoon almond extract**

¾ **cup whipping cream**

½ **cup ground almonds (from about 2½ ounces unblanched whole almonds)**

Unsweetened whipped cream, for serving (optional)

The Night Before

■ In a large, deep nonreactive skillet, combine the wine, 1 cup of the sugar, the lemon juice, and zest. Scrape the seeds from the vanilla bean into the skillet; add the bean as well. Bring to a simmer, stirring until the sugar dissolves. Add the pears, cover partially, and simmer, turning the pears once or twice, until they are just tender, about 8 minutes. Remove from the heat. Let the pears cool to room temperature in the poaching liquid. Refrigerate the pears, tightly covered, in the poaching liquid.

■ Position a rack in the middle of the oven and preheat to 375 degrees F. In a shallow metal container (like a pie pan), toast the almonds, stirring them occasionally, until they are lightly and evenly browned, about 8 minutes. Remove from the pan immediately. Let cool to room temperature, wrap well, and store at room temperature.

In the Morning

■ Position a rack in the middle of the oven and preheat to 375 degrees F.

■ Drain the pears, reserving ⅓ cup of the poaching liquid. Pat the pears dry; reserve. In a small, heavy saucepan over medium heat, combine the crabapple jelly and reserved poaching liquid. Bring to a simmer and cook briskly, stirring constantly, until reduced to ½ cup, about 5 minutes. Let cool slightly. Generously brush the inside of the tart shell with the jelly mixture; reserve the remainder.

■ Arrange 10 pear halves around the inside edge of the tart shell, placing them cut sides down and stem ends toward the center. Slice the remaining 2 pear halves and arrange them in the center of the tart.

■ In a bowl, whisk together the eggs, the remaining ⅓ cup sugar, the flour, baking powder, vanilla and almond extracts, and salt. Gradually whisk in the cream. Stir in the ground almonds. Pour the filling evenly over the pears.

■ Set the tart in the oven and bake until the filling is puffed and golden, about 40 minutes. Remove from the oven and let cool on a rack to room temperature. Remove the sides of the tart pan. Slide a long, thin knife between the bottom of the tart and the bottom of the pan. Carefully transfer the tart to a flat plate.

■ Rewarm the remaining jelly mixture. Carefully brush it evenly over the top of the tart, using it all. Sprinkle the toasted almonds over the top of the tart.

■ Slice and serve the tart, spooning a dollop of whipped cream beside each portion, if desired.

Baked Tart Shell

Makes one 10-inch tart shell

■ In a food processor, combine the flour and salt and pulse to blend. Add the butter and shortening and cut them into the flour with short pulses of power until a coarse meal forms. With the motor running, gradually add the ice water through the feed tube, stopping when moist clumps of dough form. Lightly flour a work surface. Turn out the dough, gather it into a ball, and flatten it slightly. Wrap tightly in plastic and chill for 1 hour.

■ On a lightly floured work surface, roll out the dough into a 12-inch round. Transfer the dough to a fluted 10-inch tart pan with 1¼-inch sides and a removable bottom. Trim and finish the edge. Chill the tart shell for 30 minutes.

■ Position a rack in the middle of the oven and preheat to 400 degrees F. Line the tart shell with waxed paper, fill it with dried beans or pie weights, and bake it for 10 minutes. Remove the weights and paper and bake until the pastry has lost its raw look and the crust is golden, about 6 minutes. Cool on a rack to room temperature.

■ The shell can be prepared up to 24 hours in advance. Wrap tightly and store at room temperature.

■■ Note: To measure the flour, stir it in the canister with a fork to lighten, then spoon into a dry-measure cup and sweep level.

2 cups unbleached all-purpose flour, plus flour for the work surface (see Note)

¼ teaspoon salt

8 tablespoons (1 stick) chilled unsalted butter, cut into small pieces

¼ cup chilled solid vegetable shortening, cut into small pieces

About ⅓ cup ice water

Cold Plum and White Wine Soup with Blueberries

Serves 6

You may serve a chilled fruit soup as a first course (brunch is one meal where this works), but I think my plum soup, at least, is best as dessert. Accompany the soup with gingersnaps, and for a little added panache, splash several tablespoons of sparkling white wine (it need not be the best Champagne) into each bowl just before garnishing and serving. Or omit the sour cream and float a small scoop of lemon sorbet in each bowl.

2½ pounds ripe, juicy red plums such as Santa Rosa, pitted and coarsely chopped
1½ cups medium-dry white wine
1½ cups fresh orange juice
About 1 cup sugar
1 cinnamon stick, 2 inches long
6 whole cloves
¾ cup sour cream, whisked until smooth, for garnish (optional)
Blueberries, picked over, for garnish

The Night Before

■ In a large, nonreactive saucepan over medium heat, combine the plums, wine, orange juice, ¾ cup of the sugar, the cinnamon stick, and cloves. Bring to a simmer, then cover partially, and cook, stirring once or twice, until the plums are very tender, about 25 minutes. Discard the cinnamon stick and cloves.

■ Force the soup through a food mill fitted with the medium blade, or purée in a food processor. Taste and adjust the seasoning, adding up to ¼ cup more sugar (the soup will taste less sweet when cold). Let cool completely, cover, and refrigerate.

In the Morning

■ Ladle the soup into chilled serving dishes. Decoratively drizzle the sour cream over the soup, if desired. Scatter blueberries over each serving, and serve immediately.

Deep-Dish Raspberry and Black Cherry Pie

Serves 6 to 8

The two crimson fruits baked here under a thick, tender crust are at their best in early summer, and when combined they somehow manage to taste even greater than the sum of their impressive, individual flavors. Since both fruits are also available frozen and unsweetened, the pie can be served at other times of the year as well, when its rich berried taste and fragrance are equally welcome. In any season, serve it warm, and top each portion with a scoop of premium vanilla ice cream.

■ Pit the fresh cherries, if you are using them, but leave them whole. In a large bowl, stir together the cherries, raspberries, any juices, the 1 cup sugar, flour, lemon juice, vanilla, and cinnamon. Let stand at room temperature for 20 minutes.

■ Position a rack in the middle of the oven and preheat to 400 degrees F.

■ Spoon the pie filling and any juices into a shallow 6-cup baking dish (such as a 9-by-13-inch oval gratin dish). On a lightly floured work surface, roll out the pie pastry into an oval slightly larger than the top of the baking dish (the dough will be thick). Trim the dough to fit the dish, then decoratively flute the edges. Carefully place the oval of dough atop the filling in the dish.

■ Bake the pie for 15 minutes. In a small bowl, stir together the beaten egg and water. Brush the egg mixture generously over the crust. Evenly sprinkle the crust with the remaining 2 teaspoons sugar.

■ Return the pie to the oven, lower the temperature to 375 degrees F, and bake until the crust is golden brown and the filling is bubbling, another 25 to 30 minutes. Remove from the oven and let the pie stand on a rack for up to 30 minutes. Serve warm, accompanied with scoops of the ice cream.

2 pounds fresh sweet black cherries, or 1½ pounds individually quick-frozen unsweetened black cherries, thawed, with their juices

4 cups fresh raspberries, picked over, or about 1 pound individually quick-frozen raspberries, thawed, with their juices

1 cup plus 2 teaspoons sugar

⅓ cup unbleached all-purpose flour, plus flour for the work surface

3 tablespoons fresh lemon juice

2 teaspoons vanilla extract

½ teaspoon ground cinnamon

Rich Pie Pastry (recipe follows), softened slightly

1 egg, well beaten

1 tablespoon water

About 1½ pints premium vanilla ice cream, softened slightly, for serving

Rich Pie Pastry

Makes crust for one deep dish pie

2 cups unbleached all-purpose flour
   (see Note)
¼ teaspoon salt
½ cup solid vegetable shortening,
   chilled, cut into small pieces
4 tablespoons (½ stick) chilled
   unsalted butter, cut into small
   pieces
About ⅓ cup ice water

■ In a food processor, combine the flour and salt and pulse to blend. Add the shortening and butter and cut them into the flour with short pulses of power until a coarse meal forms. With the motor running, gradually add the ice water through the feed tube, stopping when moist clumps of dough form. Lightly flour a work surface.

■ Turn out the dough, gather it into a ball, and flatten it slightly. Wrap tightly in plastic and refrigerate for at least 1 hour.

■■ Note: To measure the flour, stir it in the canister with a fork to lighten, then spoon into a dry-measure cup and sweep level.

Gingery Macadamia Truffle Brownies

Makes 16

If the spirit of brunch is one of comfortable hedonism, few desserts are more appropriate than brownies. These extremely moist, ginger-spiked brownies make a fine accompaniment to festive fruit such as long-stemmed strawberries, but they're good plain, too, with nothing more than a cup of strong coffee. Note that the brownies must be chilled before cutting; it's best to bake them one day in advance of serving.

Room-temperature unsalted butter
   for the baking pan, plus 12
   tablespoons (1½ sticks) unsalted
   butter, cut into pieces
4 ounces unsweetened baking
   chocolate, chopped
1 teaspoon instant coffee powder
3 eggs
1½ cups packed light brown sugar
2 teaspoons vanilla extract
¼ teaspoon salt
1 cup unbleached all-purpose flour
   (see Note)
1 cup chopped macadamia nuts
¼ cup minced crystallized ginger

The Night Before

■ Position a rack in the middle of the oven and preheat to 350 degrees F. Butter an 8-by-8-inch metal baking pan (if using glass, lower the oven temperature by 25 degrees).

■ In the top pan of a double boiler, combine the butter, chocolate, and coffee powder. Place over hot water and cook, stirring, just until melted and smooth. Remove from the heat and let cool to room temperature, stirring occasionally.

■ In a large bowl, whisk the eggs. Whisk in the sugar, vanilla, and salt. Fold in the chocolate mixture. Add the flour and stir until almost combined. Add the nuts and ginger and stir until just combined. Pour the batter into the prepared pan.

■ Bake the brownies until the edges look done but the center remains moist and unset, about 25 minutes. Remove from the oven and let cool on a rack to room temperature. Cover and refrigerate. (The brownies must be chilled for at least 5 hours before proceeding.)

In the Morning

■ Turn out the uncut brownies onto a work surface. With a long, sharp knife, trim away about ½ inch of the dry edge. Cut the remaining brownie square into 16 equal pieces. Let the brownies come to room temperature before serving.

■■ Note: To measure the flour, stir it in the canister with a fork to lighten, then spoon it into a dry-measure cup and sweep level.

Desserts

The Real Ambrosia

Serves 8

In the last century, before it became a gloppy, overdressed production number complete with sour cream and miniature marshmallows, ambrosia was a pristine dessert, celebrating then-novel tropical fruits. The light, refreshing genuine article is worth reviving, and is particularly nice after a rich brunch. Serve crisp ladyfingers or plain butter cookies as accompaniment.

The Night Before

■ Position a rack in the middle of the oven and preheat to 375 degrees F. Spread the coconut in a thin layer in a shallow metal baking dish (like a pie pan) and toast it, stirring once or twice, until lightly and evenly browned, about 10 minutes. Let cool completely, then wrap airtight and store at room temperature.

In the Morning

■ With a serrated knife, cut a thick slice off the top and bottom of each orange, exposing the flesh. With the knife cut down the sides of each orange, following the curve of the fruit and removing all the orange peel and bitter white pith. Cut the oranges crosswise into ½-inch-thick rounds.

■ Arrange the orange rounds, slightly overlapping them, on a large platter. Arrange the pineapple slices around the edges of the platter. Cover tightly with plastic wrap and refrigerate until cold, at least 30 minutes or for up to 1½ hours.

■ Uncover the fruit. Dust the fruit with the confectioners' sugar, using it all. Sprinkle the coconut evenly over all. Serve immediately.

⅔ cup flaked sweetened coconut

6 large oranges

1 ripe medium pineapple, quartered lengthwise, cored, peeled, and sliced crosswise

2 tablespoons confectioners' sugar, in a small sieve

Orange-Blackberry Gratins

Serves 4

Whether the orange curd is homemade or a premium jarred brand from your gourmet shop, the quick little dessert produced by spreading it over gratin dishes of fresh berries and then running them under the broiler will be utterly delicious. (Just avoid curds with a lot of dubious flavors and artificial colors in them, some of which have sweet, homestyle labels clearly designed to deceive.) Raspberries can be substituted or mixed with the blackberries. Serve a plain butter cookie on the side.

■ Position the rack about 5 inches from the broiler and preheat.

■ Divide the blackberries in a single layer among 4 shallow, broilerproof gratin dishes about 4½ inches in diameter. Spread the orange curd over the berries, dividing it equally.

■ Set the gratin dishes under the broiler and cook, watching carefully to avoid burning, until the curd is lightly browned around the edges and the berries begin to render their juices, about 4 minutes.

■ Remove from the oven and let the gratins stand on a rack for at least 15 minutes. Serve warm or cool, garnished with a sprig of mint, if desired.

About 1 pound blackberries, picked over

1⅓ cups homemade orange curd (page 73) or purchased orange or lemon curd

4 fresh mint sprigs, for garnish (optional)

MOSTLY POTENT POTABLES

6

A Very Good Bloody Mary

Serves 6

Not quite classic, since it seems to me horseradish is a recent addition to the formula, these cocktails nevertheless do strike people as perfectly balanced and exactly what they had in mind when asked if they wanted a Bloody Mary. Like chili con carne, this very good drink tends to get micromanaged, usually by men, and can often be too hot, too boozy, or so thick with horseradish as to be chewable—surprises of the sort one doesn't need early in the day. Avoid those errors by making these and you'll never go wrong. Start with chilled ingredients, and you can serve the drinks immediately, or mix everything up and refrigerate overnight (warm ingredients melt the ice and dilute the drink).

1 can (46 ounces) best-quality tomato juice, chilled
1¾ cups lemon vodka, chilled
¼ cup fresh lemon juice
3 tablespoons Worcestershire sauce
1½ tablespoons prepared horseradish
1 tablespoon hot-pepper sauce such as Tabasco
2 teaspoons soy sauce
Ice cubes
6 lemon wedges

■ In a tall pitcher, stir together all the ingredients except the ice and lemon wedges. Adjust the seasoning (hot sauces vary widely; Tabasco is among the hottest). Fill tall 12-ounce glasses with ice. Pour the tomato mixture over the ice. Squeeze a lemon wedge into each drink and serve immediately.

Ramos Gin Fizzes

Serves 4

One of the very few successful early-in-the-day uses for gin (the Singapore Sling, page 138, is another), this cocktail was trademarked in 1935 by The Fairmount Hotel in New Orleans. Citrusy, frosty, and on the light side, it's just right before a big southern brunch.

1½ cups chilled milk
½ cup plus 2 tablespoons gin
¼ cup confectioners' sugar
3 tablespoons fresh lemon juice
2 tablespoons fresh lime juice
1 egg white
1 teaspoon orange flower water
Ice cubes

■ Working in batches if necessary, combine all the ingredients over ice in a cocktail shaker. Shake well, and then strain into 10-ounce glasses, preferably tumblers. Serve immediately.

Champagne Cocktails

Beyond the basic glass of bubbly, there are a number of interesting cocktails that embellish but otherwise minimally tamper with Champagne's essential taste and effervescence. Some hosts find them simply more festive and glamorous than plain Champagne; others recognize that they are an economical way of serving less-than-spectacular (but still decent) bubbly to a crowd. Here are several favorites. Each recipe serves one.

Classic Champagne Cocktail

- Moisten a cube of sugar with a few drops of Angostura bitters. Drop it into a Champagne flute. Add 1/2 cup chilled Champagne and garnish with a twist of lemon.

Kir Royale

- Measure a dollop (between ½ and 1 teaspoon) crème de cassis into a Champagne flute. Add ½ cup chilled Champagne.

Kir Imperiale

- Substitute a raspberry liqueur like Chambord for the crème de cassis in Kir Royale.

Mimosa

- Measure ¼ cup chilled fresh orange juice into a Champagne flute. Add about 2 tablespoons chilled Champagne and stir. Add 6 more tablespoons chilled Champagne and serve immediately without stirring.

Katherine Kagel's Blood Orange Mimosa

- Substitute blood orange juice for regular orange juice in Mimosa.

Bellini

- Measure about ¼ cup puréed fresh peach (preferably a white peach such as Babcock) or peach nectar into a Champagne flute. Add about 2 tablespoons chilled Champagne and stir. Add 6 more tablespoons chilled Champagne and serve without stirring.

Three-Fruit Licuado with Rum

Serves 6 to 8

Licuados are refreshing Mexican fruit-and-milk drinks, especially enjoyed at breakfast or as a cooling midday quaff. With the addition of a good bit of rum, licuados also make fine, light brunch cocktails. With experience you can improvise licuados based upon whatever ripe, juicy fruits are in peak condition. Until then, try this tropical concoction.

2 cups cut-up pineapple (1-inch chunks)
1½ cups amber rum
2 cups cut-up cantaloupe (1-inch chunks)
About 2 cups milk
2 cups cut-up mangoes (1-inch chunks; from about 2 mangoes)
About ⅓ cup sugar
Ice cubes (optional)
Lime wedges, for serving

The Night Before

■ In a food processor, combine the pineapple and rum and process until smooth. Transfer to a large sieve set over a bowl. In the same processor, purée together the cantaloupe and 1 cup of the milk. Transfer to the sieve. Add the mangoes, the remaining milk, and the sugar to the processor and purée. Transfer the mango to the sieve. With a spatula, force the licuado through the sieve. Cover and refrigerate overnight.

In the Morning

■ Taste the licuado and adjust the seasoning. Pour into tall glasses over ice, if desired. Squeeze a lime wedge into each drink and serve immediately.

Singapore Slings

Serves 4

This tall, fruity drink was invented at the Raffles Hotel in Singapore just after the turn of the century. Here is the version currently served at the recently renovated Raffles.

2 cups pineapple juice, chilled
¼ cup gin
¼ cup cherry brandy
¼ cup fresh lime juice
3 tablespoons grenadine
2 tablespoons Cointreau
2 tablespoons Benedictine
½ teaspoon Angostura bitters
Ice cubes
1 thin slice unpeeled fresh pineapple, quartered
4 maraschino cherries

■ Working in batches if necessary, combine the pineapple juice, gin, cherry brandy, lime juice, grenadine, Cointreau, Benedictine, and bitters over ice in a cocktail shaker. Shake well, and then strain into tall glasses. Skewer 1 wedge of pineapple and 1 cherry onto each of 4 cocktail picks, garnish each drink with 1 pick, and serve immediately.

A Great Cup of Cocoa

Serves 4 to 6

Cocoa is a morning beverage, hot chocolate more of a midday pick-me-up-cum-dessert, at least as I see it. Making cocoa from scratch lets you enrich it with cream, if desired, and adjust the amount of cocoa and sugar to your personal taste level. Marshmallows, too, are subject for individual adjustment (I'm for 'em). Start with this fairly straightforward recipe, which is adapted from the one on the Hershey's cocoa box. Who would know better?

■ In a heavy saucepan, stir together the cocoa powder and sugar. Gradually whisk in the hot water. Stir in the milk, cream, and salt, and set the pan over medium heat. Cook, stirring often, until just steaming (do not boil).

■ Remove from the heat and stir in the vanilla. For a frothy beverage, beat the cocoa with a hand-held electric mixer for about 1 minute. Ladle the cocoa into mugs, top with marshmallows, if desired, and serve immediately.

¼ **cup lightly packed unsweetened cocoa powder**
⅓ **cup sugar**
⅓ **cup hot water**
3 **cups milk**
1 **cup whipping cream, or 1 additional cup milk**
Pinch of salt
½ **teaspoon vanilla extract**
Miniature marshmallows (optional)

Rum Milk Punch

Serves 8

A slight twist on the classic brandy milk punch, this smooth, cool, not-too-potent potable, with its slight touch of coffee liqueur, is just right early in the day.

■ In a blender, combine half of each ingredient. Cover and blend on high until the punch is smooth and frothy. Divide the punch among 4 tall glasses. Serve immediately. Repeat with the remaining ingredients.

2½ **cups chilled milk**
1 **cup amber rum**
½ **cup Tia Maria coffee liqueur**
2 **tablespoons vanilla extract**
¼ **teaspoon freshly grated nutmeg**
10 **ice cubes**

Baja Breeze

Serves 1

I developed this drink at my Manhattan chili restaurant several years ago when beer cocktails seemed to be heading toward trendhood. The buzz was premature, but now that brew pubs are sweeping the land, and people in general want to drink lighter, beer cocktails are back. This is a good and zesty one, based on the Mexican drink called *sangrita*. Make it with a mellow amber beer such as Dos Equis. Those who don't care about drinking light and who aren't driving may want to use it as a chaser for tequila shots.

¼ **cup fresh orange juice, chilled**
¼ **cup tomato juice, chilled**
Dash of hot-pepper sauce such as Tabasco
Ice cubes
About ½ cup beer, chilled
Lime wedge

■ In a tall 12-ounce glass, stir together the orange juice, tomato juice, and hot-pepper sauce. Fill the glass with ice. Slowly pour in the beer until the glass is full. Squeeze the wedge of lime into the cocktail and serve immediately.

Toddy Coffee Shake

Serves 1

The Toddy coffee maker is a slow drip system that makes a coffee-flavored concentrate. Brewed without heat, it is mellow but very strong, and produces an instant cup of coffee when mixed with hot water. When diluted with cold milk and served over ice, it is almost the very best thing to drink on a very hot day. Topping said beverage with a scoop of premium ice cream—coffee, chocolate, or vanilla—makes a good thing great, and can just as easily serve as dessert after a summertime brunch. Look for a Toddy setup at better coffee bean stores.

1 **cup chilled milk**
¼ **cup Toddy coffee concentrate, chilled**
Ice cubes
1 **large scoop coffee, chocolate, or vanilla ice cream**

■ In a tall 12-ounce glass, combine the milk, coffee concentrate, and enough ice to fill the glass. Stir well. Top with the ice cream and serve immediately, with a long spoon.

A Wonderful Cup of Coffee

- The best coffee comes from freshly roasted, estate-grown beans of the general type known as arabica, ideally purchased from a company that roasts its own or from a specialty retailer with a high turnover. (Most supermarket coffees, especially canned coffees, are made from inferior robusta beans.)

- Once roasted, coffee beans quickly begin to go stale. Once ground, coffee goes stale even faster. Buy only whole beans and store those not to be used up within a week in the freezer in an airtight container.

- Grind the beans just before brewing the coffee. Use cold fresh water, and if your water supply has off flavors, consider buying one of the simple charcoal drip–pitcher filter systems on the market.

- For brewing, coffee experts most often recommend the drip system (automatic or otherwise) and the French press, such as the plunger-style Melior system. The carafe should be absolutely clean, free from any residual coffee oils (which quickly turn rancid) as well as the taste of dishwashing soap.

- Grind the beans to the fineness recommended by the manufacturer of the coffee system you are using. Measure the coffee accurately—the industry standard is two tablespoons (one coffee-measuring spoonful) to each six ounces of water (most big coffee mugs are twelve or thirteen ounces). If you are using the proper grind, this will produce a well-balanced, full-strength cup of coffee. Adjust future pots for your personal taste.

- Water for perfect brewing should be just below boiling. Some automatic coffee makers never reach this temperature. Rating guides (like *Consumer Affairs*) can help you make the most informed purchase.

- If you have brewed more than one cup, store the remainder in a Thermos. Sitting on a hot plate will quickly ruin the wonderful coffee that you have spent so much time achieving.

Table of Equivalents

The exact equivalents in the following tables have been rounded for convenience.

US/UK	Metric
oz=ounce	g=gram
lb=pound	kg=kilogram
in=inch	mm=millimeter
ft=foot	cm=centimeter
tbl=tablespoon	ml=milliliter
fl oz=fluid ounce	L=liter
qt=quart	

Weights

US/UK	Metric
1 oz	30 g
2 oz	60 g
3 oz	90 g
4 oz (¼ lb)	125 g
5 oz (⅓ lb)	155 g
6 oz	185 g
7 oz	220 g
8 oz (½ lb)	250 g
10 oz	315 g
12 oz (¾ lb)	375 g
14 oz	440 g
16 oz (1 lb)	500 g
1½ lb	750 g
2 lb	1 kg
3 lb	1.5 kg

Oven Temperatures

Fahrenheit	Celsius	Gas
250	120	½
275	140	1
300	150	2
325	160	3
350	180	4
375	190	5
400	200	6
425	220	7
450	230	8
475	240	9
500	260	10

Liquids

US	Metric	UK
2 tbl	30 ml	1 fl oz
¼ cup	60 ml	2 fl oz
⅓ cup	80 ml	3 fl oz
½ cup	125 ml	4 fl oz
⅔ cup	160 ml	5 fl oz
¾ cup	180 ml	6 fl oz
1 cup	250 ml	8 fl oz
1½ cups	375 ml	12 fl oz
2 cups	1 L	32 fl oz

Length Measures

US/UK	Metric
⅛ in	3 mm
¼ in	6 mm
½ in	12 mm
1 in	2.5 cm
2 in	5 cm
3 in	7.5 cm
4 in	10 cm
5 in	13 cm
6 in	15 cm
7 in	18 cm
8 in	20 cm
9 in	23 cm
10 in	25 cm
11 in	28 cm
12 in	30 cm

Mail-Order Sources

Grains

Arrowhead Mills, Inc.
Box 866
Hereford, TX 79045
(806) 364-0730
Assorted organic grains and flours

Calloway Gardens Country Store
Highway 27
Pine Mountain, GA 31822
(404) 663-2281, ext. 5100
Speckled heart hominy grits

Dean & DeLuca
560 Broadway
New York, NY 10012
(212) 431-1691
Assorted grains and flours, many organic

Lundberg Family Farms
5370 Church Street
Richvale, CA 95974
(916) 882-4551
Organic fancy rice blends

The Santa Fe School of Cooking and
Market
116 West San Francisco Street
Santa Fe, NM 87501
(505) 983-4511
Blue cornmeal

Vermont Country Store
Weston, VT 05161
(802) 824-3184
Assorted grains and flours

Walnut Acres
Penns Creek, PA 17862
(717) 837-3874
Assorted organic grains and flours

Wolferman's
1 Muffin Lane
P.O. Box 15913
Shawnee Mission, Kansas 66285-5913
(800) 999-0169
English muffins

Hot Sauces

Mo Hotta Mo Betta
Box 4136
San Luis Obispo, CA 93403
(800) 462-3220

Coyote Cocina
1364 Rufina Circle #1
Santa Fe, NM 87501
(800) 866-4695

Maple Syrup

Everett and Kathryn Palmer
Route 1, Box 246
Waitsfield, VT 05673-9711
(802) 496-3696

Meat and Fish

Aidells Sausage Company
1625 Alvarado Street
San Leandro, CA 94577
1 (800) 546-5795

Burger's Smokehouse
RFD 3 Box 126
Highway 87 South
California, MN 65081-9903
(314) 796-4111
*City and country hams, bacon, peppered
bacon, sausages, smoked turkey*

Roy L. Hoffman and Sons Smoked Bacon
Route 6, Box F5
Hagerstown, MD 21740
(800) 356-2332

Jugtown Mountain Smokehouse
77 Park Avenue
Flemington, NJ 80022
(201) 782-2421
*Dry-cured, nitrite-free, hardwood-smoked
bacon; smoked ham, turkey, and chicken*

Nueske's Hillcrest Farm Meats
RR 2
Wittenberg, WI 54499
(800) 382-2266
*Apple wood smoked hams, turkeys, and
bacon*

Ducktrap River Smoked Fish
RFD 2, Box 378
Lincolnville, ME 04849
(800) 828-3825
Smoked trout, scallops, mussels, and salmon

Coffee Beans

The Coffee Connection
Six Drydock Avenue
Boston, MA 02201
(800) 284-5282

Starbucks
2203 Airport Way South
P.O. Box 34510
Seattle, WA 98124
(800) 782-7282

Peets Coffee and Tea
P.O. Box 8247
Emeryville, CA 94662
(800) 999-2132